LAST LAUGHS

CARTOONS ABOUT AGING, RETIREMENT . . .
AND THE GREAT BEYOND

EDITED BY

MORT GERBERG

SCRIBNER
New York   London   Toronto   Sydney

SCRIBNER
A Division of Simon & Schuster, Inc.
1230 Avenue of the Americas
New York, NY 10020

First Scribner hardcover edition October 2007

SCRIBNER and design are trademarks of Macmillan Library Reference USA, Inc., used under license by Simon & Schuster, the publisher of this work.

For information about special discounts for bulk purchases, please contact Simon & Schuster Special Sales: 1-800-456-6798 or business@simonandschuster.com.

Text set in Adobe Caslon

Manufactured in the United States of America

1   3   5   7   9   10   8   6   4   2

Library of Congress Control Number: 2007061802

ISBN-13: 978-1-4165-5100-3
ISBN-10: 1-4165-5100-X

Page 193 is an extension of the copyright page.

Dedicated to Bud Handelsman and all the other classic cartoonists who are already mining funny material in The Great Beyond . . .
. . . and to the rest of us who, someday, will.

CONTENTS

Introduction by Mort Gerberg

ix

CARTOONS BY

George Booth; Roz Chast; Frank Cotham; Leo Cullum; Matthew Diffee;
Mort Gerberg; Sam Gross; J. B. Handelsman; Sidney Harris; Ed Koren;
Glen Le Lievre; Arnie Levin; Lee Lorenz; Marisa Acocella Marchetto;
Warren Miller; Frank Modell; Victoria Roberts; David Sipress;
Barbara Smaller; Mick Stevens; Mike Twohy; P. C. Vey;
Kim Warp; Robert Weber; Gahan Wilson;
Jack Ziegler

1

Contributors

135

Acknowledgments

189

Index

191

INTRODUCTION

Many cartoonists say they can't explain exactly how they get their ideas—and it *is* the question we're asked most often. I once heard Charles Addams, whose cartoon characters became known as the Addams Family, tell an inquiring fan, "Well now, I don't really know; I'm like a cow—I just give milk."

I remember, though, where I got the idea for this book. I was at Alta, the ski resort east of Salt Lake City. I had just completed an exhilarating day of skiing and was pulling off my boots in the lodge when suddenly the door flew open and a small man wearing an orange parka and a large portion of the mountain burst into the room, waving his arms and showering snow all around.

"Yess! *Yess!! Skied for free!*" He flung his hat and goggles against the ceiling. "Today is my eightieth birthday!" he roared. "And *I skied for free! Free at last!*" I grinned and saluted him with a raised fist. This octogenarian's achievement was a long-held goal of mine, too—to reach that age when, at some mountains, skiers may ride the lifts without paying.

I relished my memory of the exuberant eighty-year-old youngster; he made a wonderful role model. And I've spent some time thinking about aging. The fact is that aging people are remaining active and now are as likely to pursue second careers as move to sunny retirement communities with shuffleboard courts. I'm thrilled by people in all fields who have continued to do their thing regardless of their age: Matisse inventing remote-control collage while in bed at eighty-five; "Doc" Cheatham blowing jazz trumpet at ninety-two; Eubie Blake still playing warp-speed ragtime piano at one hundred; or Bernard Baruch, who was a millionaire by age thirty, but still continued to advise U.S. presidents until his death at ninety-four.

One of my special heroes was Art Buchwald, the humorist known for his sly commentary on politics. At the age of eighty Art made headlines when he discontinued dialysis treatment for his failing kidneys and checked into a hospice in Washington, D.C. He resumed writing his syndicated column, signed a book deal, and turned the place into his private salon before moving back to Martha's Vineyard to live his final days. He taped a comedy good-bye video that opened with a head shot of him croaking, "Hi. My name is Art Buchwald, and I just died."

I have a fantasy scenario about my own demise that goes something like this: I'm ninety-nine years old and I'm *still* playing second base for *The New Yorker* softball team. My first at bat, I crack a line drive over the third baseman's head for a stand-up double. Our next batter is a lefty, so I'm not expecting him to smash a rocketlike shot toward shortstop as I'm dashing to third. When I turn to look toward the plate, the ball hits me right between the eyes and I drop like a rock. I'm dead. Just like that. *Death by Line Drive.*

A freelancer for most of my career, I am now in my seventies (wait, when did *that* happen?), and I intend to keep working as hard and as long as I can. The word *retire* is not in my vocabulary. At lunches with my fellow cartoonists, I am not surprised to hear that everyone feels the way I do. None of them has plans to retire; they all continue to draw, experiment with new media, try different creative forms, and not think too much about tomorrow. Retire from *what?* they ask. From what we love to do? What would be the point?

This collection is their response to the big three: retirement, aging, death. Cartoons about the end of life. Last laughs. Many cartoons here spin off the familiar and timeless—deathbed confessions, doctors, heaven, hell, the grim reaper, funerals—but others venture into the brave new world of the twenty-first century—cloning, cryogenic freezing, and celebrity eulogies.

These are far-reaching, outrageous, wet-right-out-of-the-pen, skewed views of people in or approaching their final years—and beyond. Almost all of the cartoons are original; they were made to order especially for this collection and have never been seen before. Several did appear previously in *The New Yorker* and were simply too good to resist.

The contributors to *Last Laughs* are some of the best single-panel cartoonists in the world. All will be familiar from the pages of *The New Yorker*. Each has a different drawing style, point of view, and sense of humor, and they span seven decades. They are in their thirties, forties, fifties, sixties, seventies, eighties, and one, the incomparable Frank Modell, is in his *ninetieth* year.

Modell, the oldest and arguably greatest living master of this art form (he's got a number of years on other senior greats you'll see here, such as George Booth, Lee Lorenz, and Bob Weber), finally gave in to my insistent entreaties and agreed to come out of his self-imposed withdrawal from active cartooning. He fretted, wrote ideas, and sketched a batch of energetic new roughs, then drew and redrew the finishes with the same compulsive tenacity and passion he had when he was twenty. *Still* the embodiment of the consummate professional, Frank Modell is what this collection is all about.

Of course, *Last Laughs* is really about the fact that everyone *will* get older and everyone *will* die—though we tend to live in denial about it. If this book has an overall message, it might be to suggest that we steer clear of the old Road of Avoidance when we're confronted with retiring, aging, and dying. One alternative approach is to embrace the concept that the end of life is a part of life and deal with it as we would with any other familiar irritation such as traffic or technology—by laughing about it.

For the best cartoons not only produce laughs, they tell truths.

And laughs last.

Mort Gerberg
New York
April 2007

CARTOONS BY

George Booth; Roz Chast; Frank Cotham; Leo Cullum; Matthew Diffee;
Mort Gerberg; Sam Gross; J. B. Handelsman; Sidney Harris; Ed Koren;
Glen Le Lievre; Arnie Levin; Lee Lorenz; Marisa Acocella Marchetto;
Warren Miller; Frank Modell; Victoria Roberts; David Sipress;
Barbara Smaller; Mick Stevens; Mike Twohy; P. C. Vey;
Kim Warp; Robert Weber; Gahan Wilson;
Jack Ziegler

"You're going to keep on looking until you find something—aren't you?"

"Line two. Someone from the 'Times' wants to punch up your obituary."

"In the new lifestyle, sixty years of age is forty and eighty is the new sixty and a hundred and fifteen years of age is the new ninety-five. Now don't that make you feel better, Uncle Spencer?"

"Well, it sure beats sitting on your duff and playing Bingo."

"I've changed my living will to a living-it-up will."

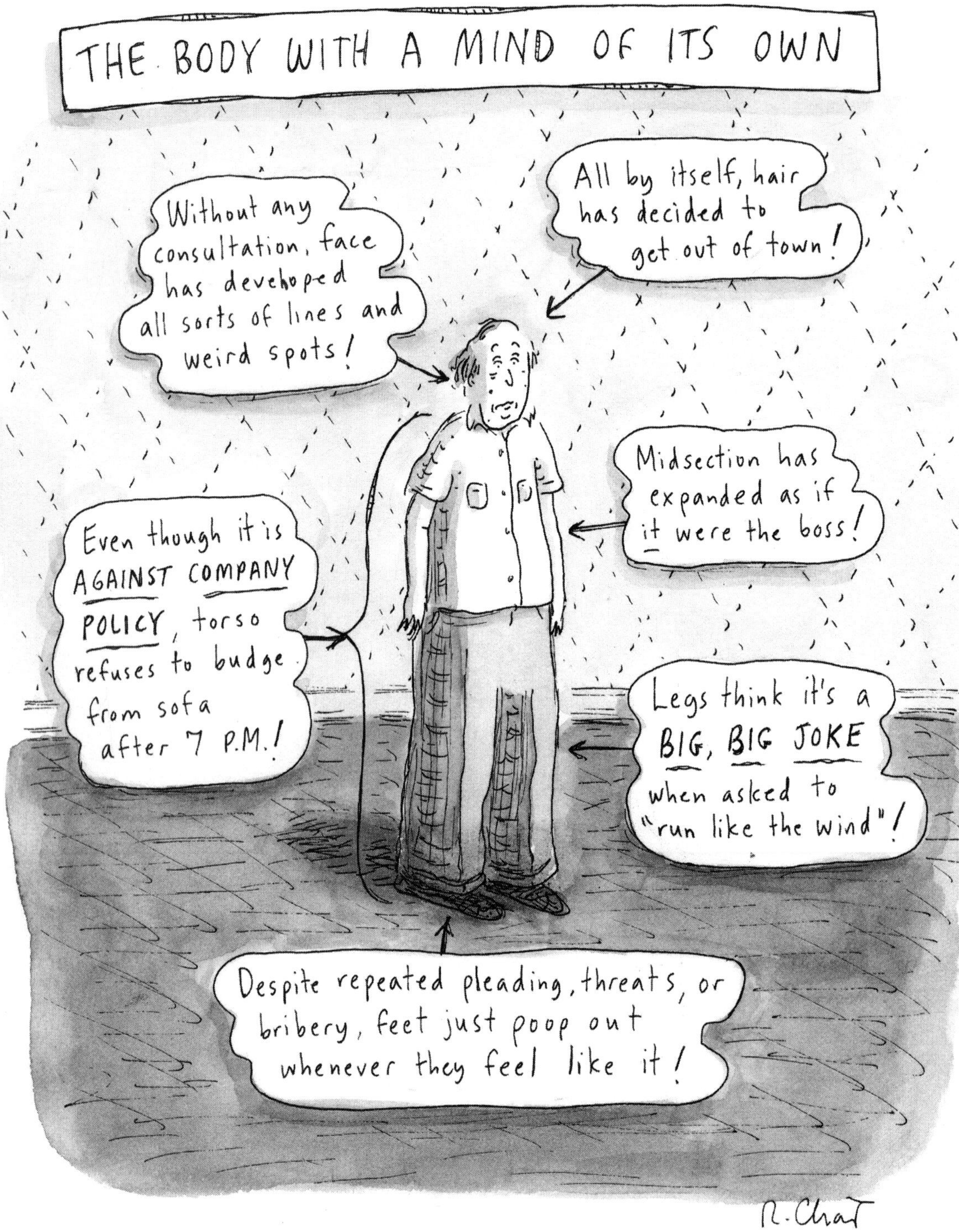
THE BODY WITH A MIND OF ITS OWN
Without any consultation, face has devehoped all sorts of lines and weird spots!
All by itself, hair has decided to get out of town!
Midsection has expanded as if it were the boss!
Even though it is AGAINST COMPANY POLICY, torso refuses to budge from sofa after 7 P.M.!
Legs think it's a BIG, BIG JOKE when asked to "run like the wind"!
Despite repeated pleading, threats, or bribery, feet just poop out whenever they feel like it!
R. Chast

"Do you have your original warranty?"

"Could you give me another hour, pal? I just took a Viagra."

"I sent your worry beads out to be re-strung."

"Irwin's deeply concerned about global warming.
He's afraid there won't be any Florida to retire to."

"Jason and I want to talk to you guys about assisted living."

"Do you think I'm too old to act my age?"

". . . and look what I have for you. It's your short-term memory."

"We're going to back off on the hormone replacement a little bit."

"I suppose now we'll all be euthanized."

"Do you think your parents still hook up?"

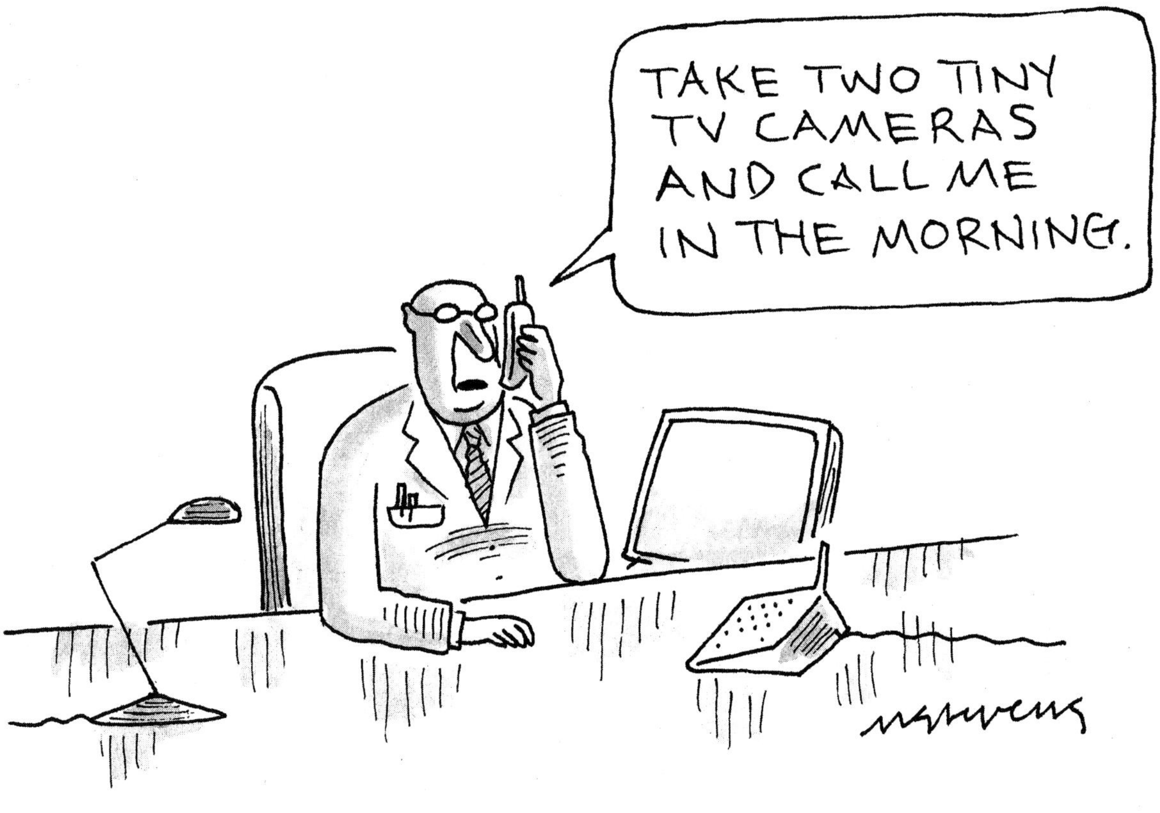
TAKE TWO TINY TV CAMERAS AND CALL ME IN THE MORNING.

THE FUTURE OF MEDICINE

"*A great catch. He's a widower, still frisky, and has fully paid-up long-term-care insurance.*"

"I'd like to be buried in this outfit, if I can lose ten pounds."

"Miss Calmon, get me everything available on cloning. Pronto!"

"These are my reading glasses. I need my sex glasses."

"Wasn't this supposed to be one of those how-to-prepare-for-retirement seminars?"

"Assisted suicide? You should live so long."

"*Shut up! Wearing ill-fitting, unlaundered, nondesigner vintage was <u>your</u> idea of Hell.*"

"I think I've lost the will to die."

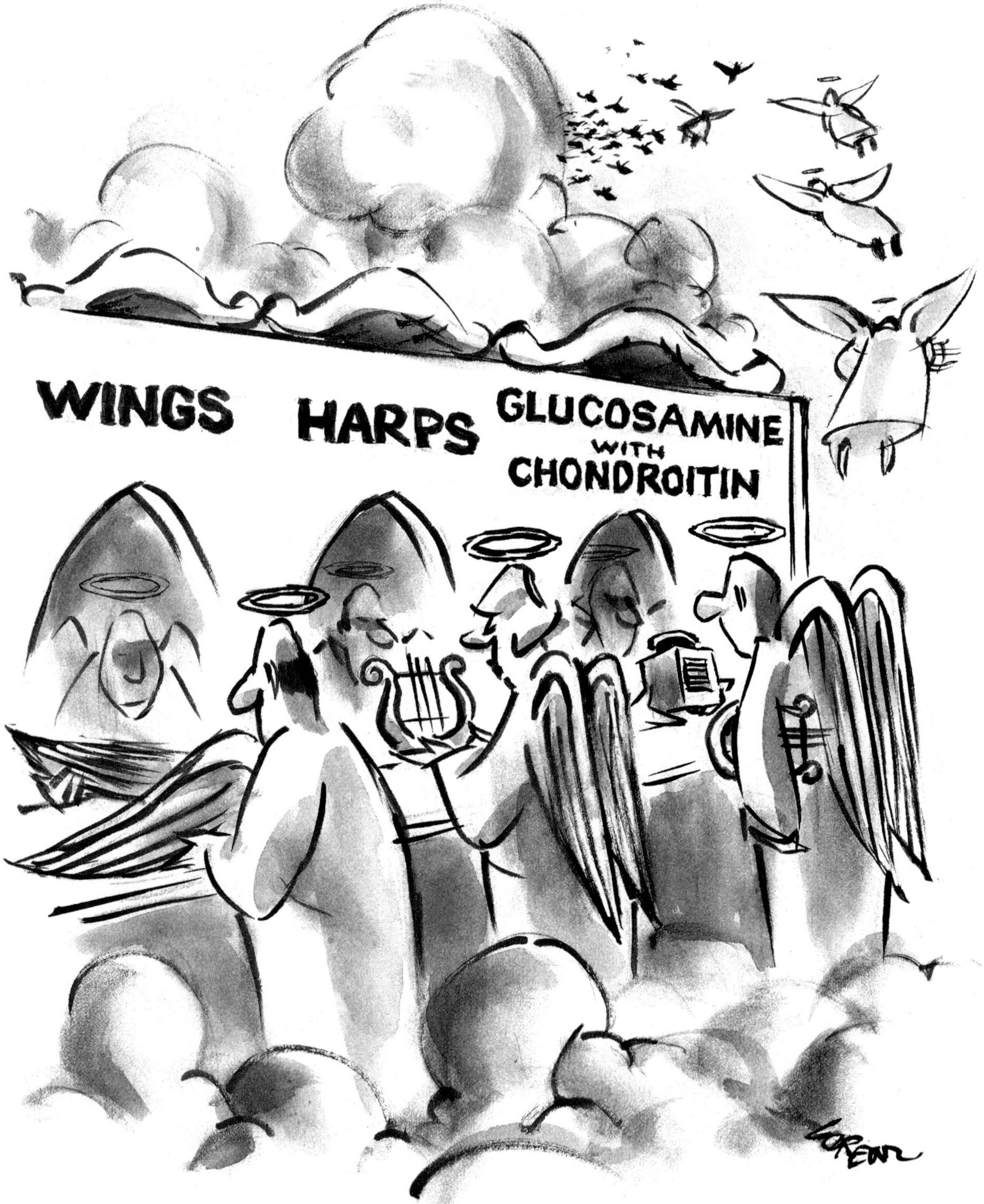
WINGS
HARPS
GLUCOSAMINE
WITH
CHONDROITIN
LORENZ

"He left his body to the Cryonics Institute, and he'll be picking up his money when he thaws out."

"I don't think of it as prison. I think of it as long-term care."

"*I went from zero to sixty a lot quicker than I expected to.*"

"All you ever hear is football, basketball, baseball—never a word about quilts."

"If there is a hereafter after the here I wonder if there is a thereafter after the hereafter yonder."

"Somehow I thought the coffee would be better."

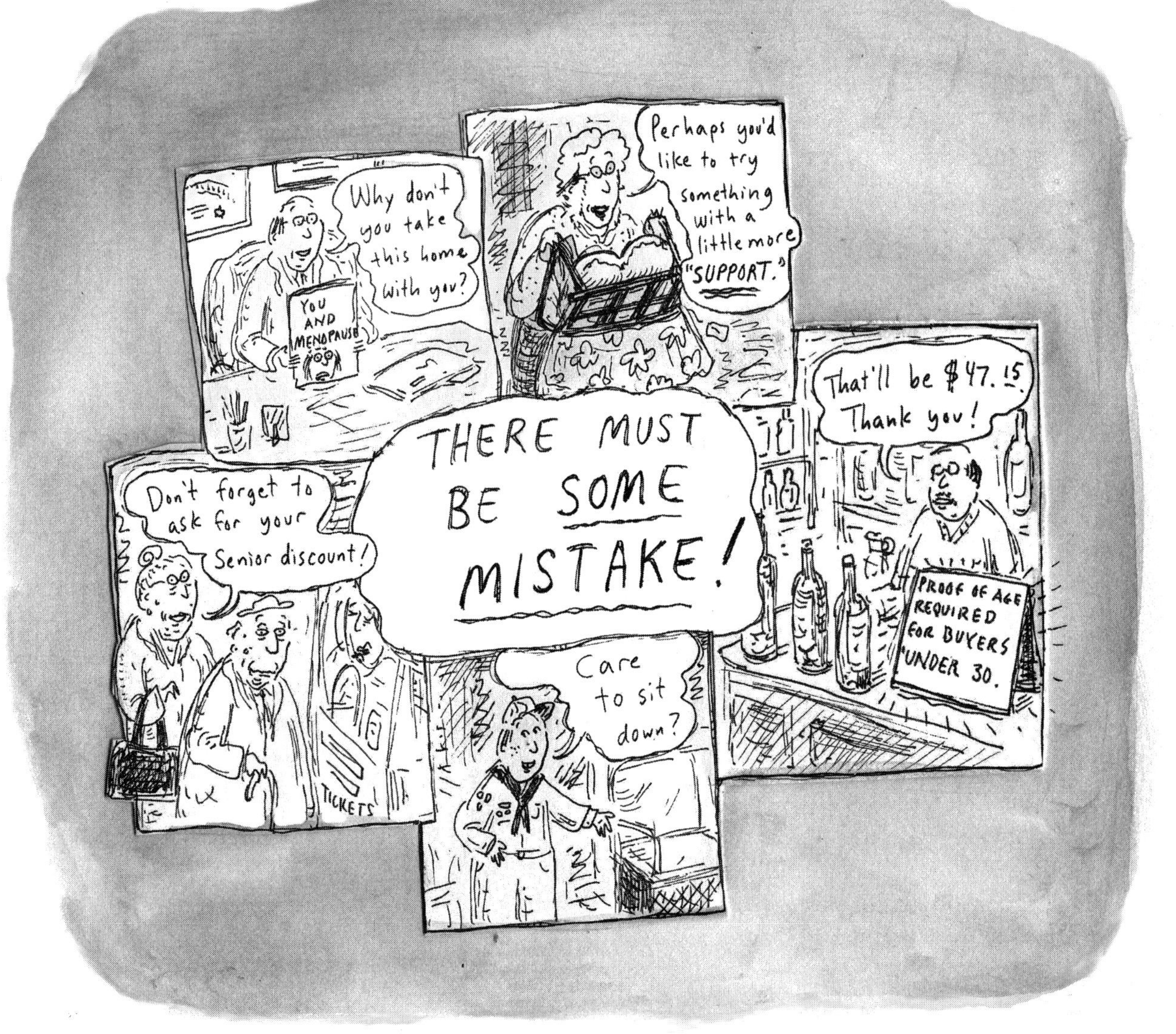
Why don't you take this home with you?
YOU AND MENOPAUSE
Perhaps you'd like to try something with a little more "SUPPORT."
That'll be $47.15 Thank you!
Don't forget to ask for your Senior discount!
THERE MUST BE SOME MISTAKE!
PROOF OF AGE REQUIRED FOR BUYERS UNDER 30.
Care to sit down?
TICKETS

"Oh, you know with Leonardo, it's never retirement, it's always reinvention."

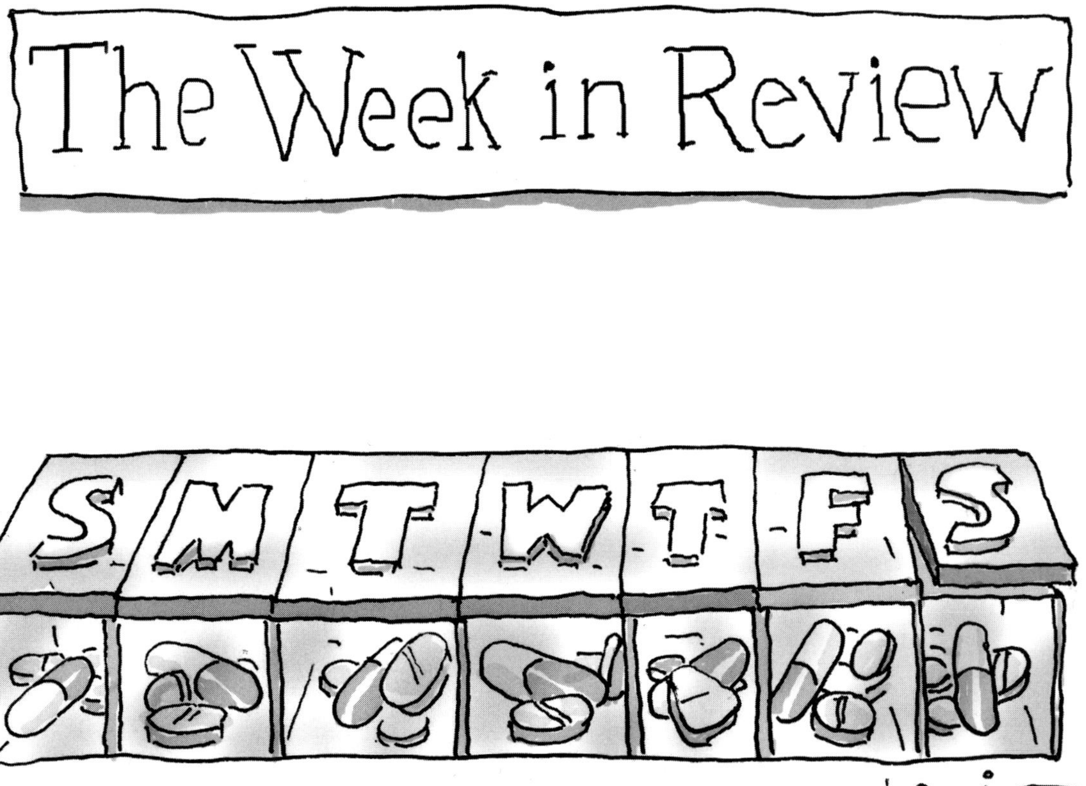
The Week in Review
S M T W T F S
Levin

*"It's so sad about Helen. Doctors have done all that they could possibly do,
but she still shows her age."*

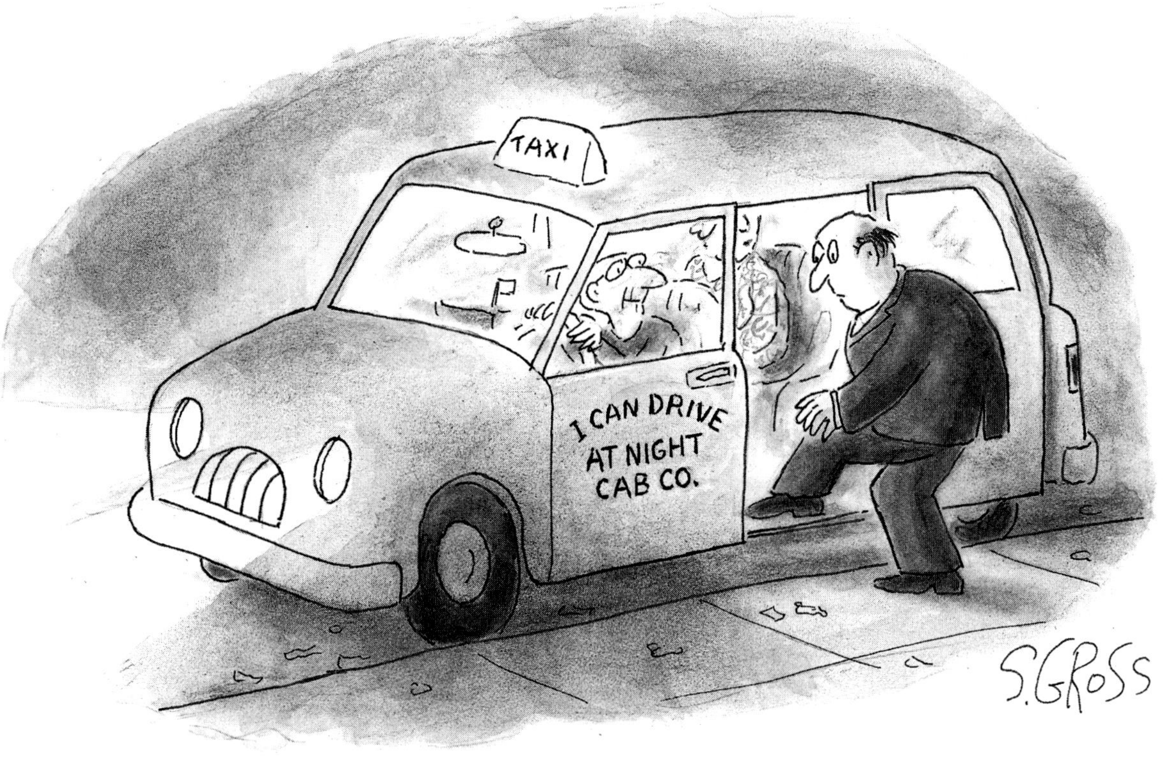
TAXI
I CAN DRIVE
AT NIGHT
CAB CO.
S.GROSS

"This one comes with a complimentary last will and testament."

"He doesn't play catch or fetch anymore. Just roll over and play dead."

You Wish

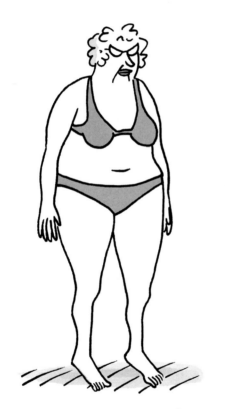

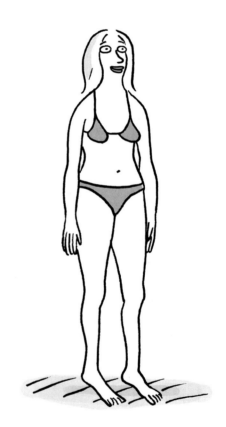

Original File   Backup File

"By this time next week, Martha will be the first Gray Panther to walk on the moon."

*"Walter's taken up magic. He knows how to get rabbits out of a hat,
but he doesn't know how to put them back in."*

"We have no mandatory retirement age, Dave, but under certain conditions
we tend to encourage people to die."

"We don't want to be a burden to you, sweetheart, but who else are we going to be a burden to?"

"Don't know about you, Ethel, but I can't seem to get used to this thong."

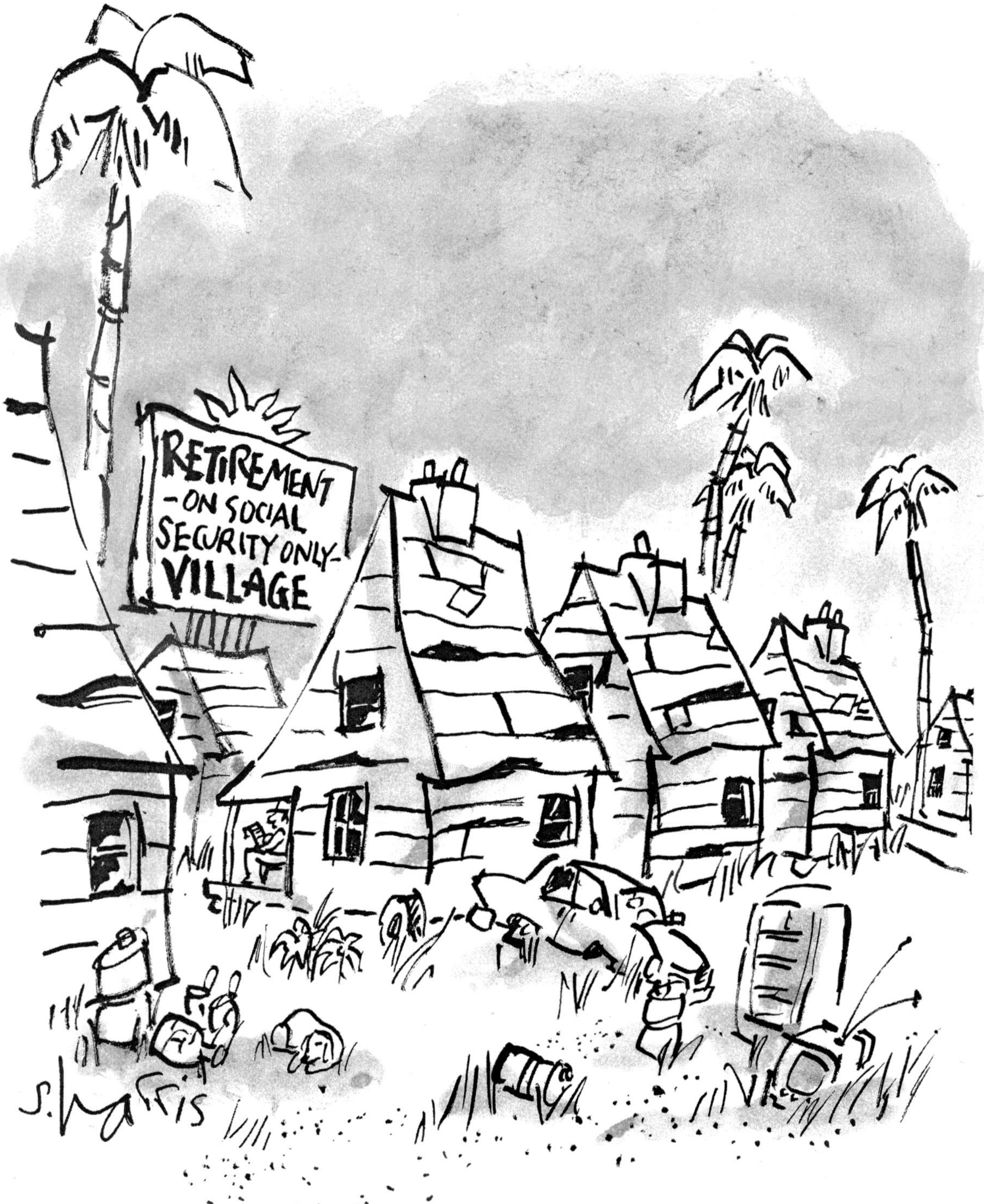
RETIREMENT
-ON SOCIAL
SECURITY ONLY-
VILLAGE
S. Harris

"I want my living will to stipulate that I spend my last hours sipping a piña colada on Maui."

"It's comforting knowing the children are finally on their own and in rehab."

"Every night they watch reruns of old 'Seinfeld' shows. Soon it may be time to take them away to the old boomers' home."

"It's spelled out quite clearly: your health plan does <u>not</u> cover metamorphosis."

"I'll tell you another thing. I outlived more doctors than you, too."

LeLIEVRE

"Grampa's secret of longevity is life-support."

BAD TIMING

TOO YOUNG FOR THE 'SIXTIES

Why won't you let me go to Woodstock? WHY ???

TOO SQUEAMISH FOR THE 'SEVENTIES

I can't believe they're doing that in public.

TOO POOR FOR THE 'EIGHTIES

the Excelsior
1 BEDROOM APTS
$600,000.00
ONLY 3 LEFT!

TOO TECHNOPHOBIC FOR THE 'NINETIES

TOO OLD FOR THE '00'S

"Before we discuss costs, are we talking the brain, the head, or the whole enchilada?"

"You're retired, Jack. Loosen your tie."

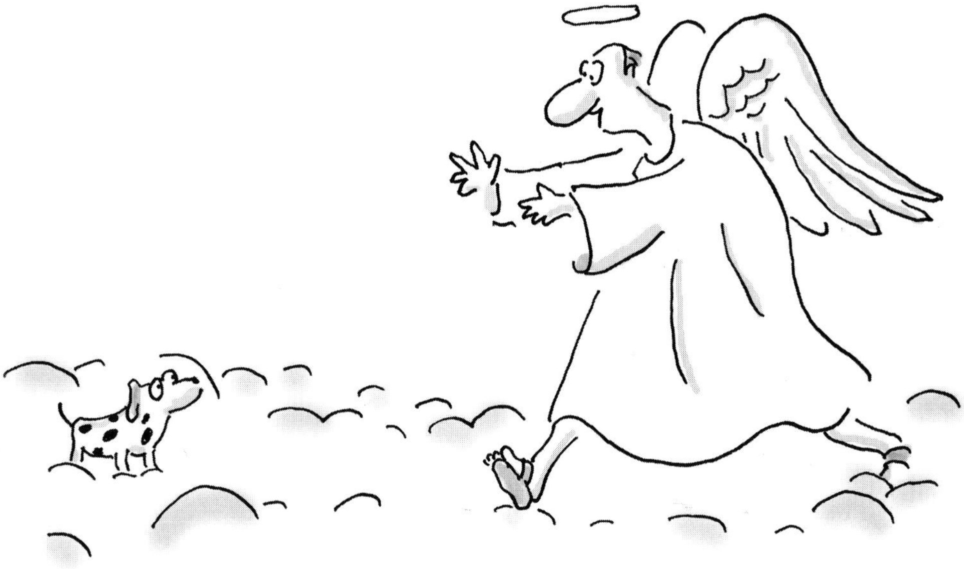

"Spot, my little dog Spot!"

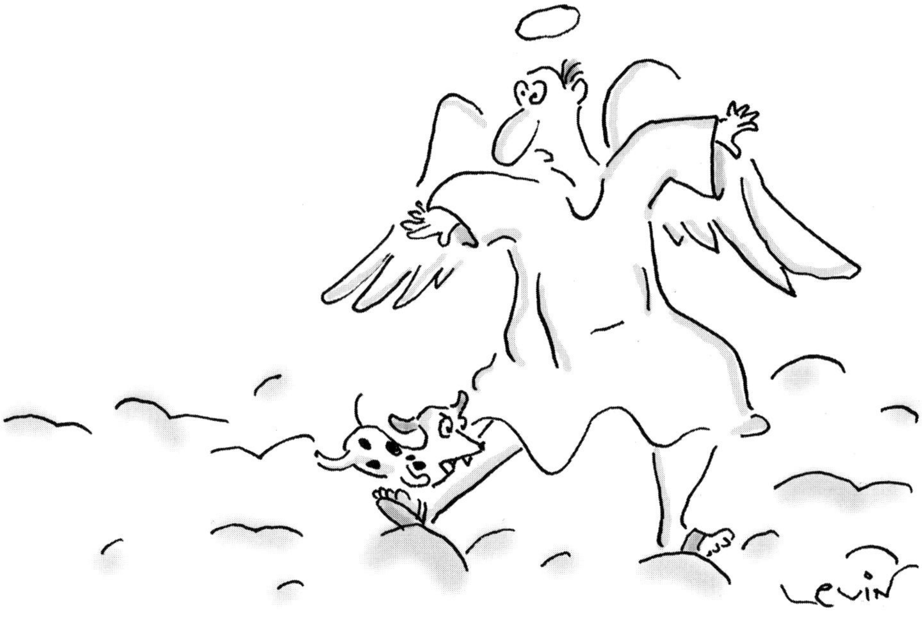
LEVIN

"Since he retired, he's been driving me nuts with his chore-ethic."

"I'm sure we can squeeze you in for this evening as long as you don't mind being naked and on fire."

MODERN RETIREMENT

Thanks to Modern Science, retirement is likely to last much longer than ever before . . .

. . . Unfortunately, recent studies show retirement is becoming increasingly boring . . .

. . . The regrettable result is that retirees hold long, one-way boring conversations with clerks in supermarkets . . .

. . . Some supermarkets have responded by installing automated clerks to bore them back, but that hasn't made things less boring . . .

... Meanwhile there has been an increase in the number of arrests of bored and boring retirees for boring policemen ...

... But this has only resulted in jails being crowded with boring people ...

... And since statistics show retirement is exclusively enjoyed by compulsive gardeners and golfers ...

... Most theologians agree the same is probably true for the Afterlife.

"*I don't know what my last words are going to be.
I just hope they have nothing to do with work.*"

"At this point in my life, I'm not so much looking for love as for next of kin."

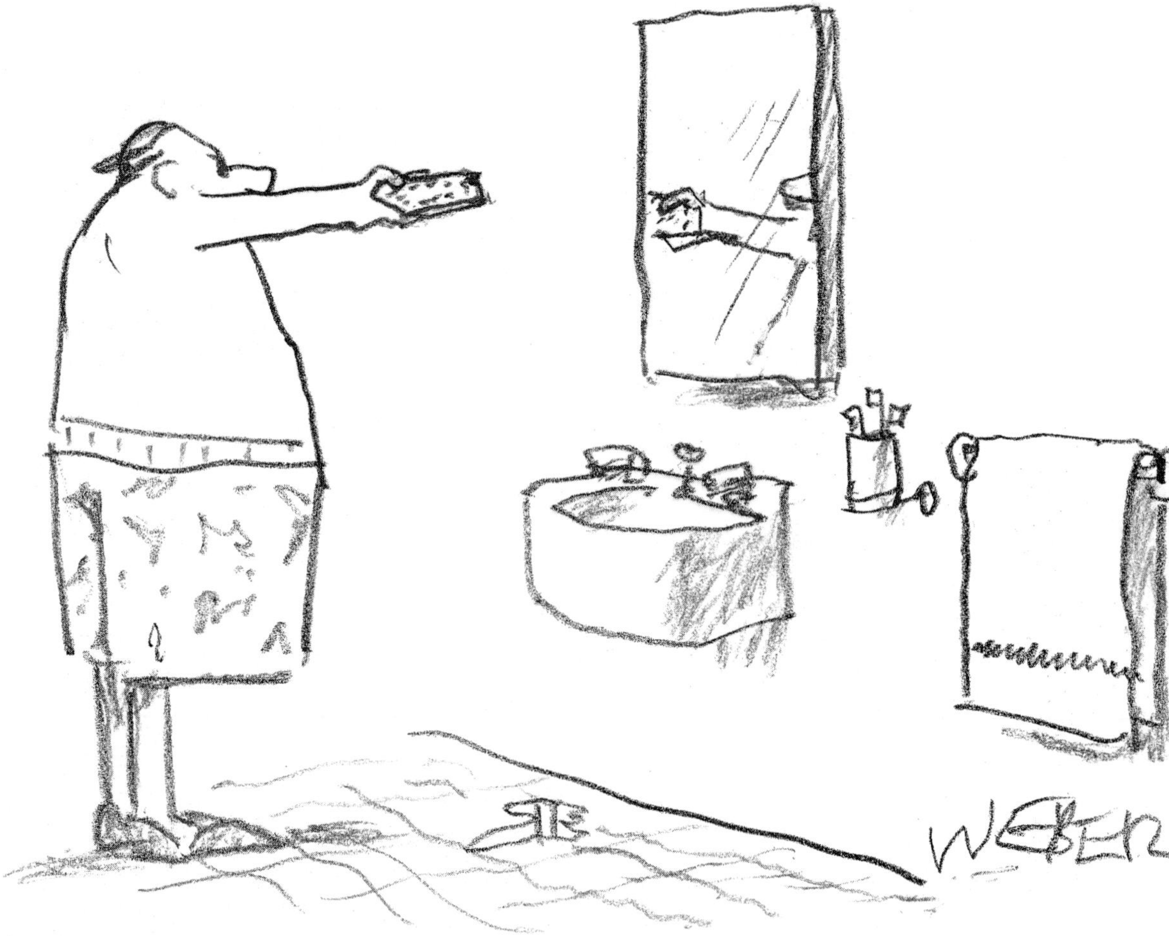
WEBER

"My inner child just turned sixty-five."

"He looked dreadful when I last saw him. Maybe I should shoot right for the sympathy cards."

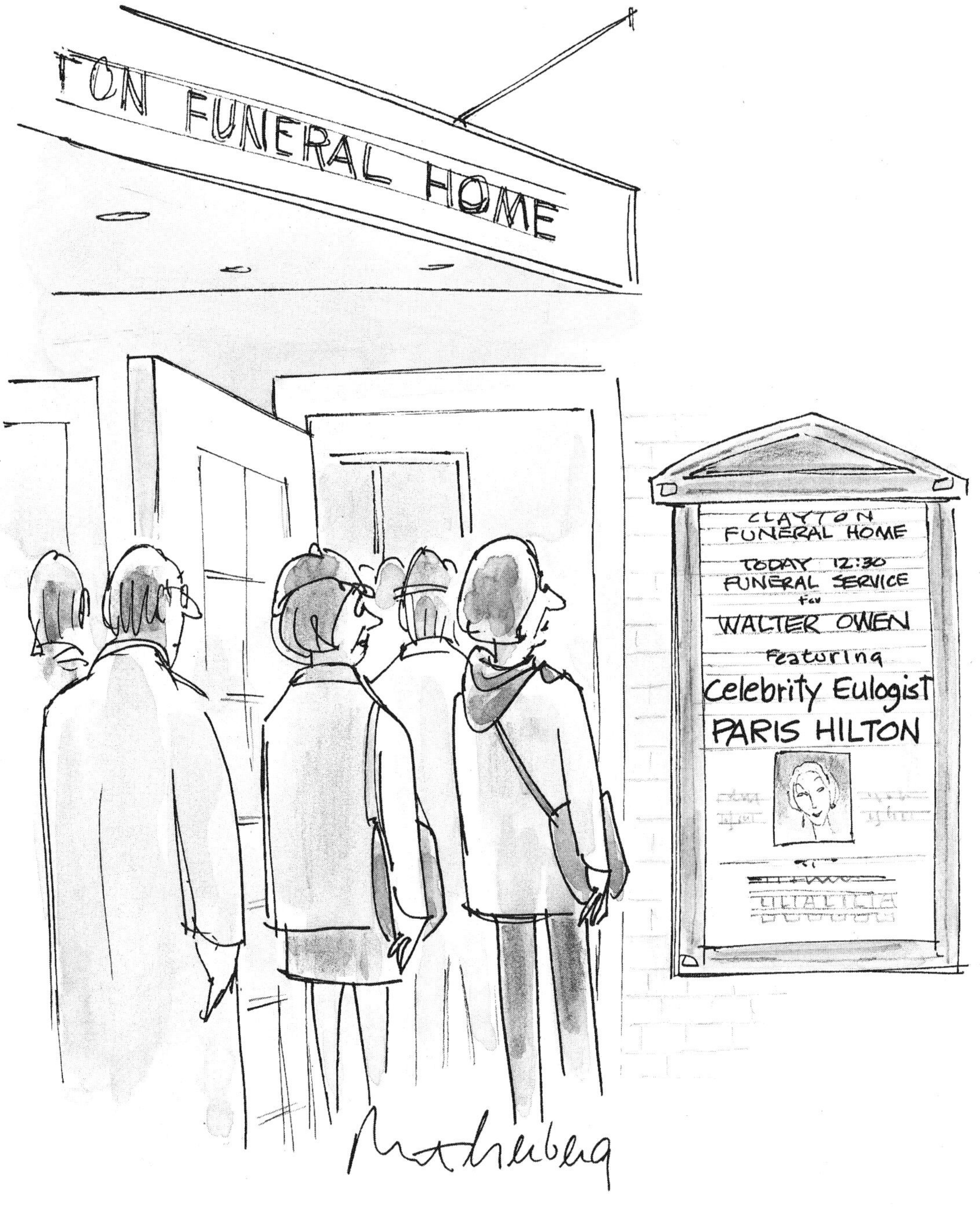
TON FUNERAL HOME
CLAYTON
FUNERAL HOME
TODAY 12:30
FUNERAL SERVICE
for
WALTER OWEN
featuring
Celebrity Eulogist
PARIS HILTON

"If you've been a circus performer you can never really retire."

"I understand old Ferguson wrote the service himself."

When Scrapbookers Die

"Quick—get the camera!"

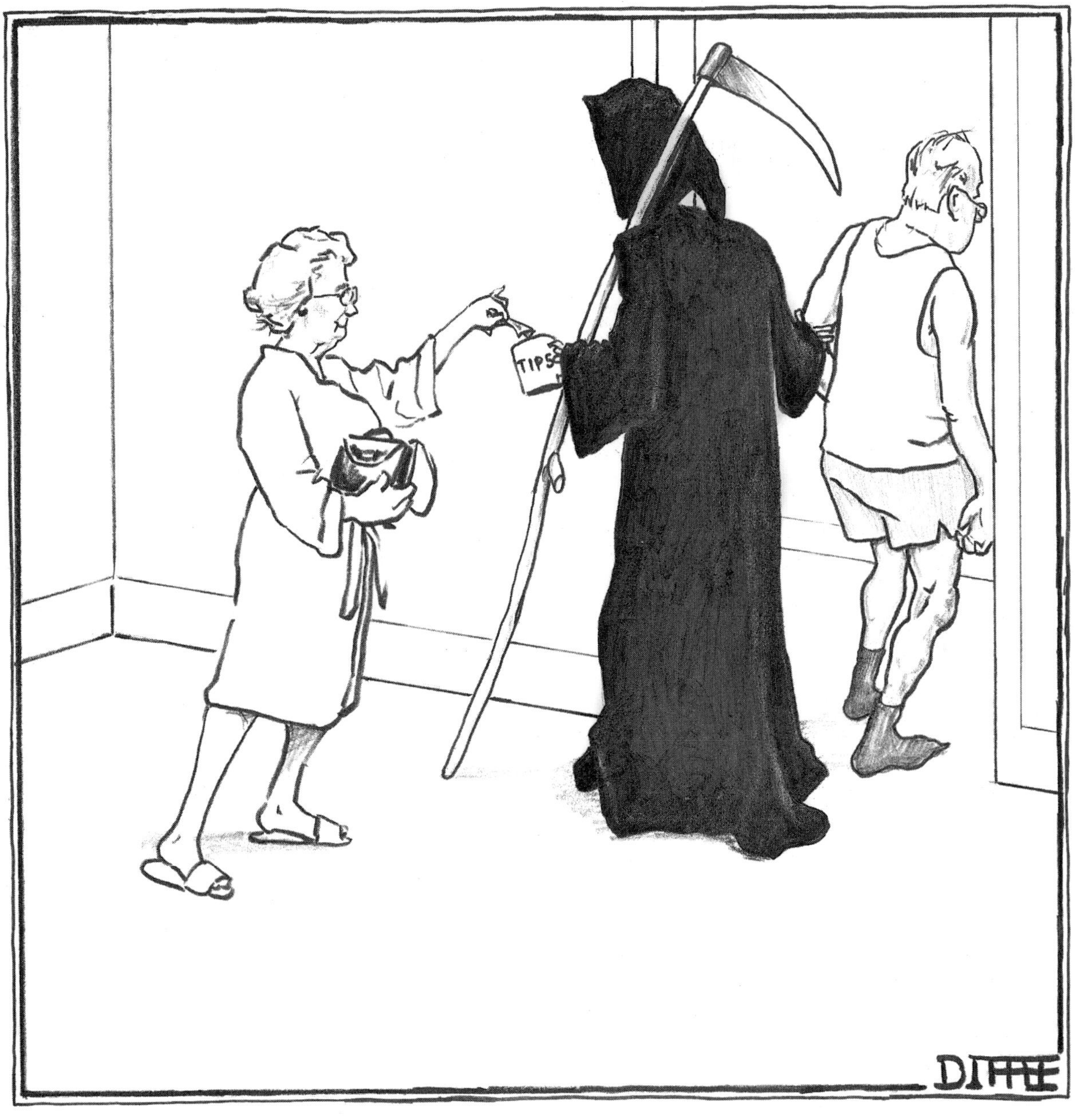
TIPS
DIFFEE

"Fill out this tag and attach it to your big toe."

"*The poor dear wanted to give his own eulogy, but I'm doing the rebuttal.*"

"If you gentlemen find the heart-healthy offerings a little dull, you might be tempted by our traditional angioplasty and triple-bypass menu."

SENIOR-CITIZEN GRAMMIES

The Least Embarrassing Relics of the '60's Award

The Most Convincing Display of Adolescent Angst Award

The How _Do_ They Manage To Stay So Youthfully Slim? Award

Special Medal of Honor for Letting It All Go To Hell

"Before we try assisted suicide, Mrs. Rose, let's give the aspirin a chance."

"I'll take this one."

"I guess I never realized that getting old was such a big part of the aging process."

"Are your ties getting wider or are you getting thinner?"

"I see it! I see it! That bright white light! Quick! Get me my straw hat, my cane, and my tap shoes!"

"As usual, Manny, you get fifteen minutes on your prostate and I get fifteen on my colon."

"Everett Klem, this is the Fat Lady, and she's about to sing for you."

"When he goes, should we tell you directly, or is there some euphemism you prefer?"

"Not much in the way of hard assets, I'm afraid, but he did leave some highly desirable organs."

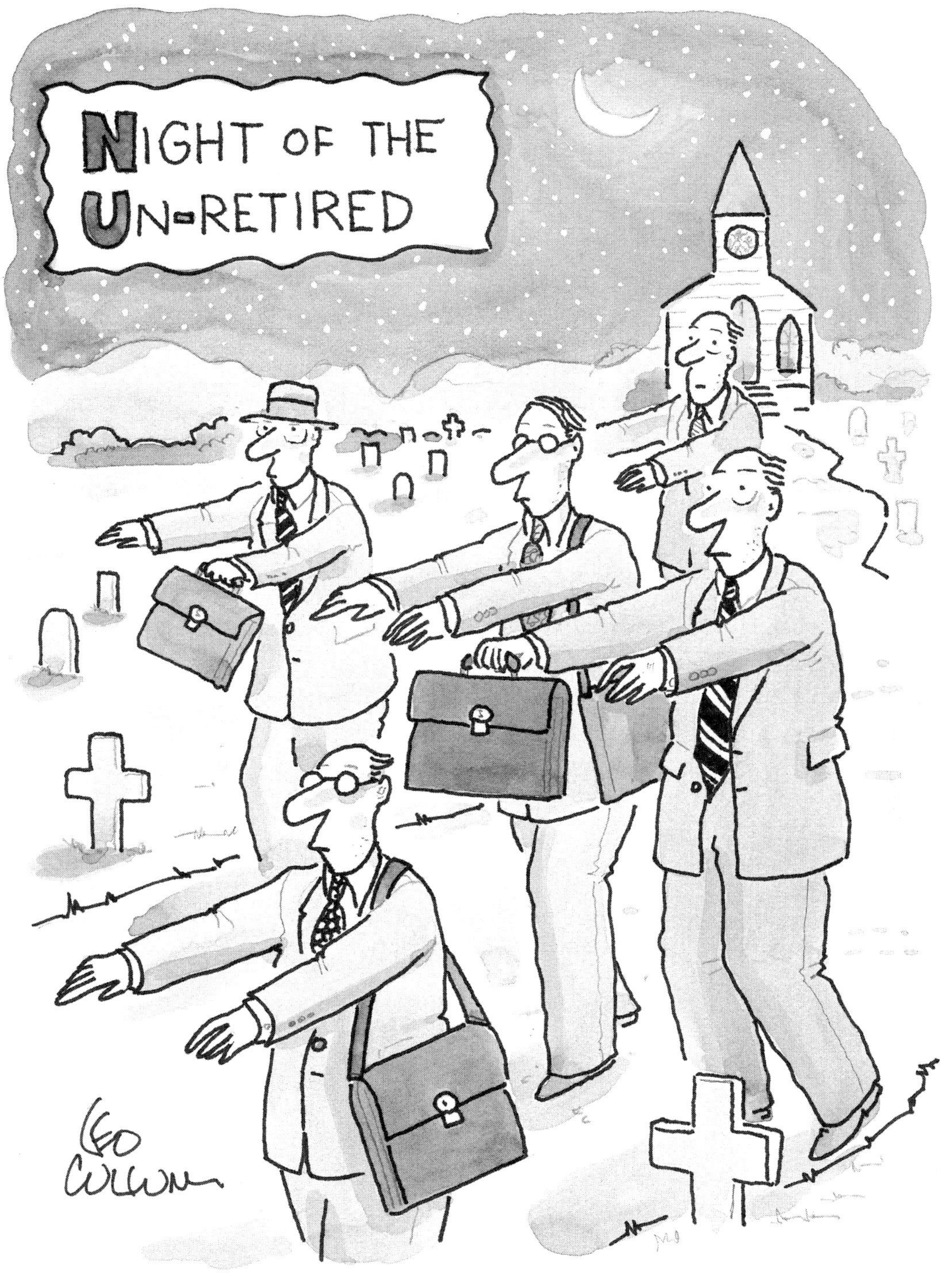
NIGHT OF THE
UN-RETIRED
LEO CULLUM

"Five hundred dollars Hodge dies before you get your Martini."

"It's the overeating that did him in. Now it's killing his pallbearers."

"This is the part about retirement I hate."

"That get–well card we sent certainly was a waste of money."

"You know what might be fun? An M.R.I."

"Change your will and leave me all your money."

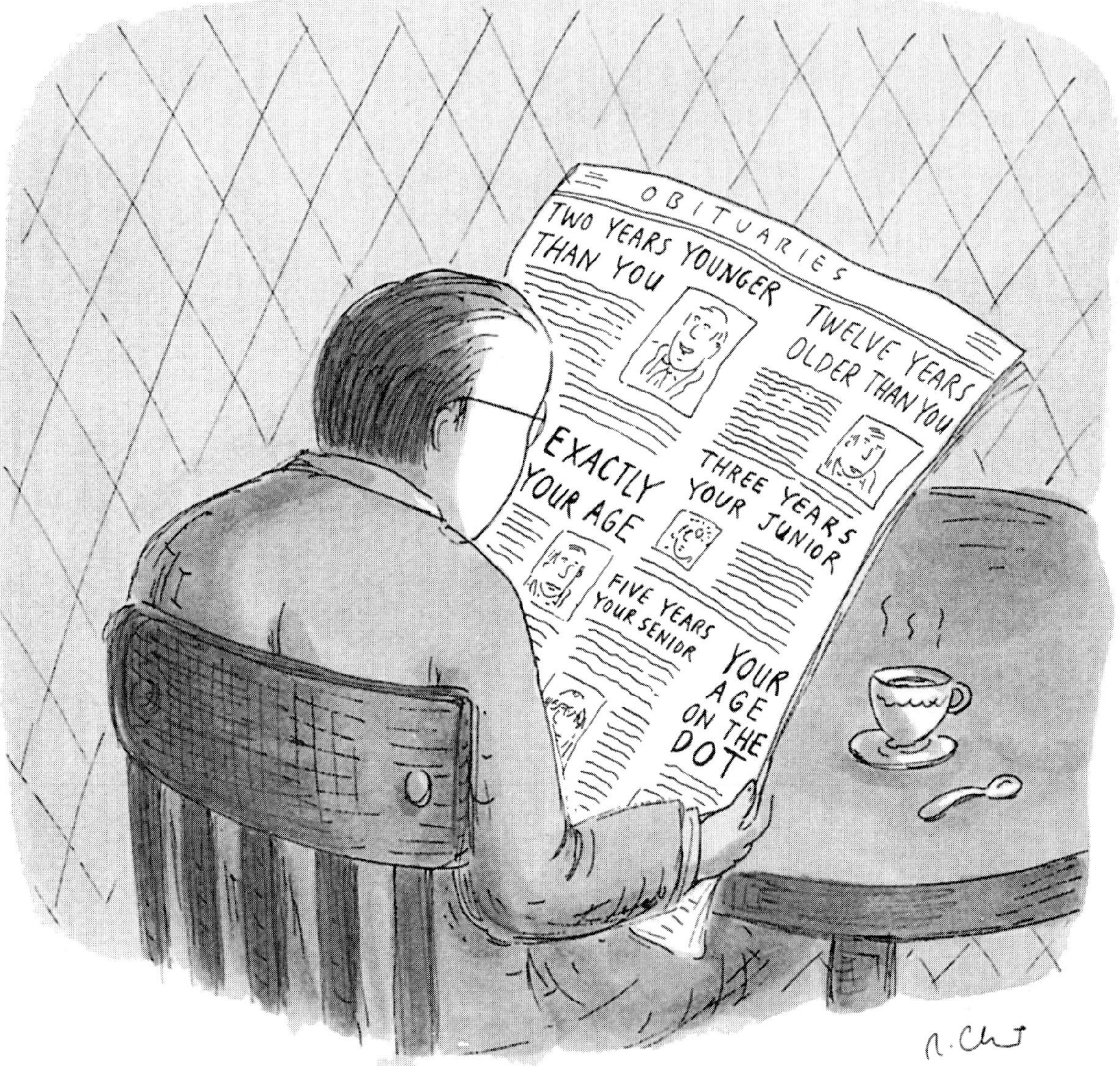
OBITUARIES
TWO YEARS YOUNGER THAN YOU
TWELVE YEARS OLDER THAN YOU
EXACTLY YOUR AGE
THREE YEARS YOUR JUNIOR
FIVE YEARS YOUR SENIOR
YOUR AGE ON THE DOT

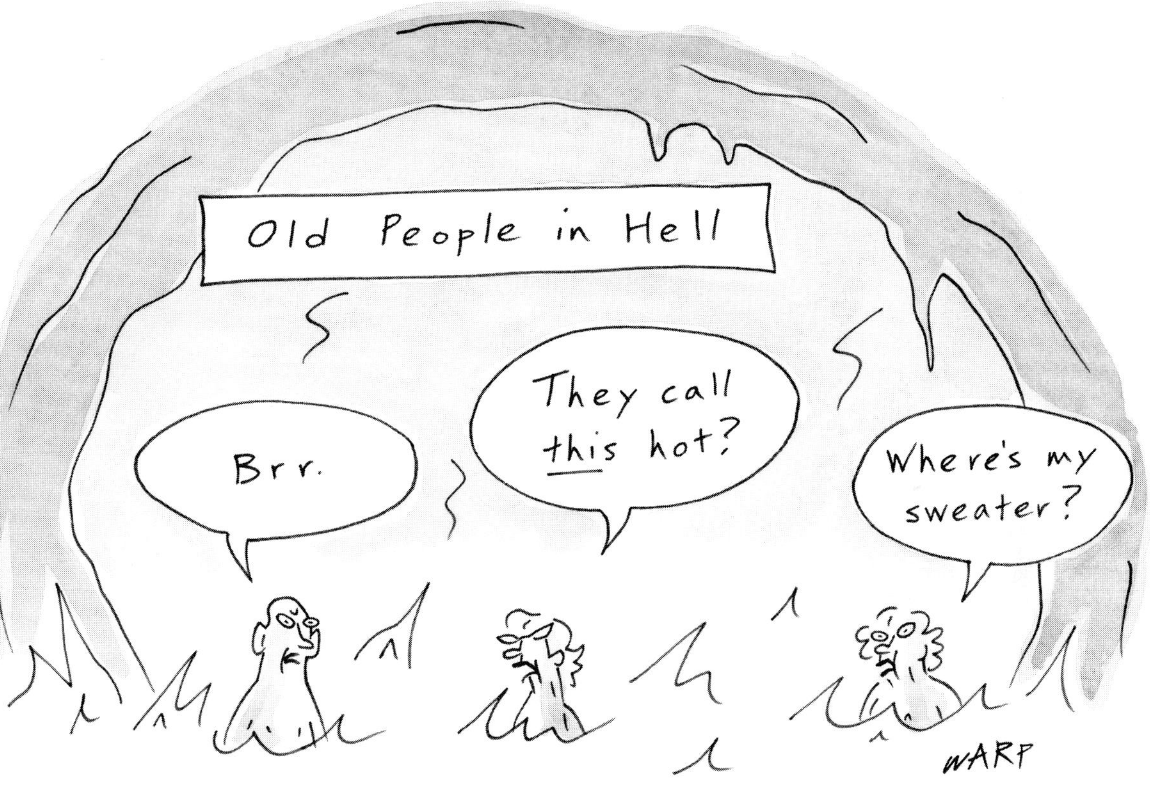
Old People in Hell
Brr.
They call this hot?
Where's my sweater?
WARP

"Of course I'm not dead! First I have to go 'AAARGH!' __Then__ I'll be dead."

"Wait, those weren't lies. That was spin!"

"If we take a late retirement and an early death, we'll just squeak by."

"Mom! Dad! You've gotten back together!"

"*. . . and finally, I'd like to read a selection of Howard's unpublished letters to the 'N.Y. Times.'*"

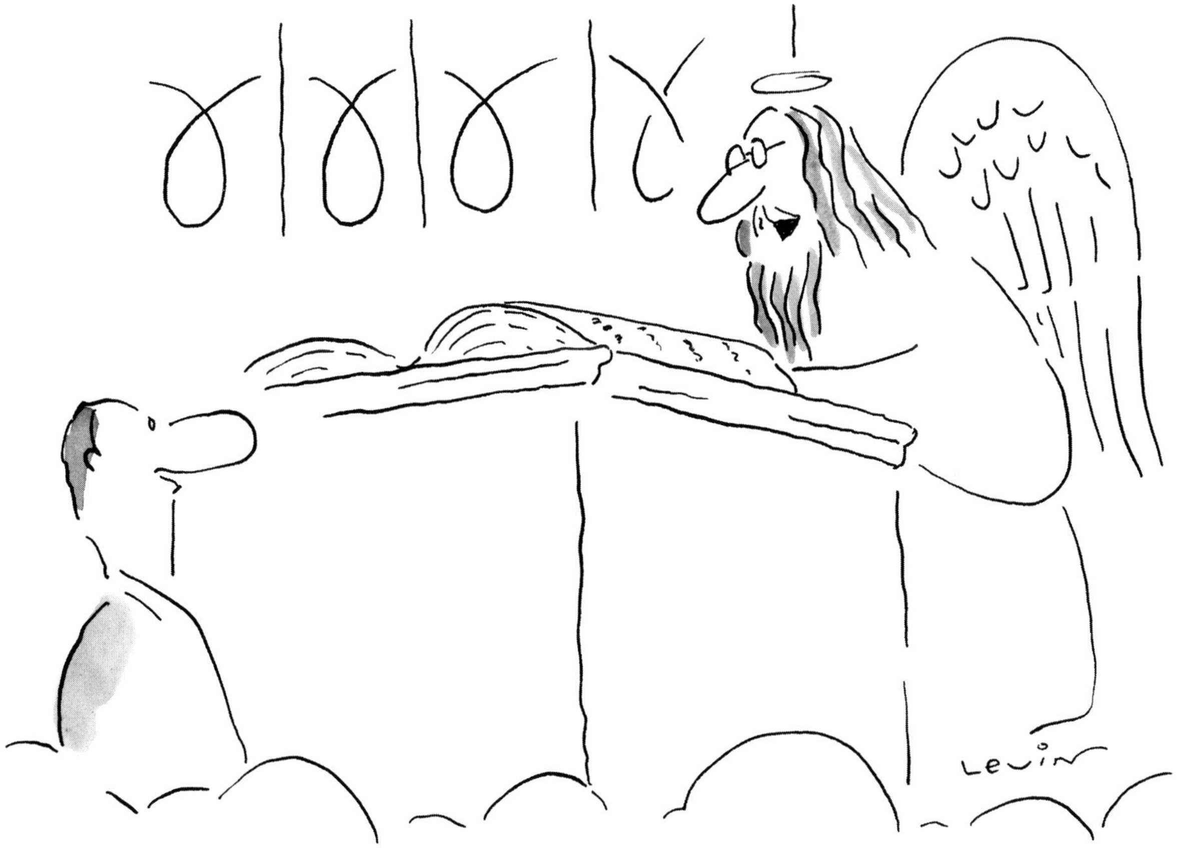
LEVIN

"User name and password?"

"*Everybody we know is here.*"

"Dead! How do you know he's dead? You're a dermatologist."

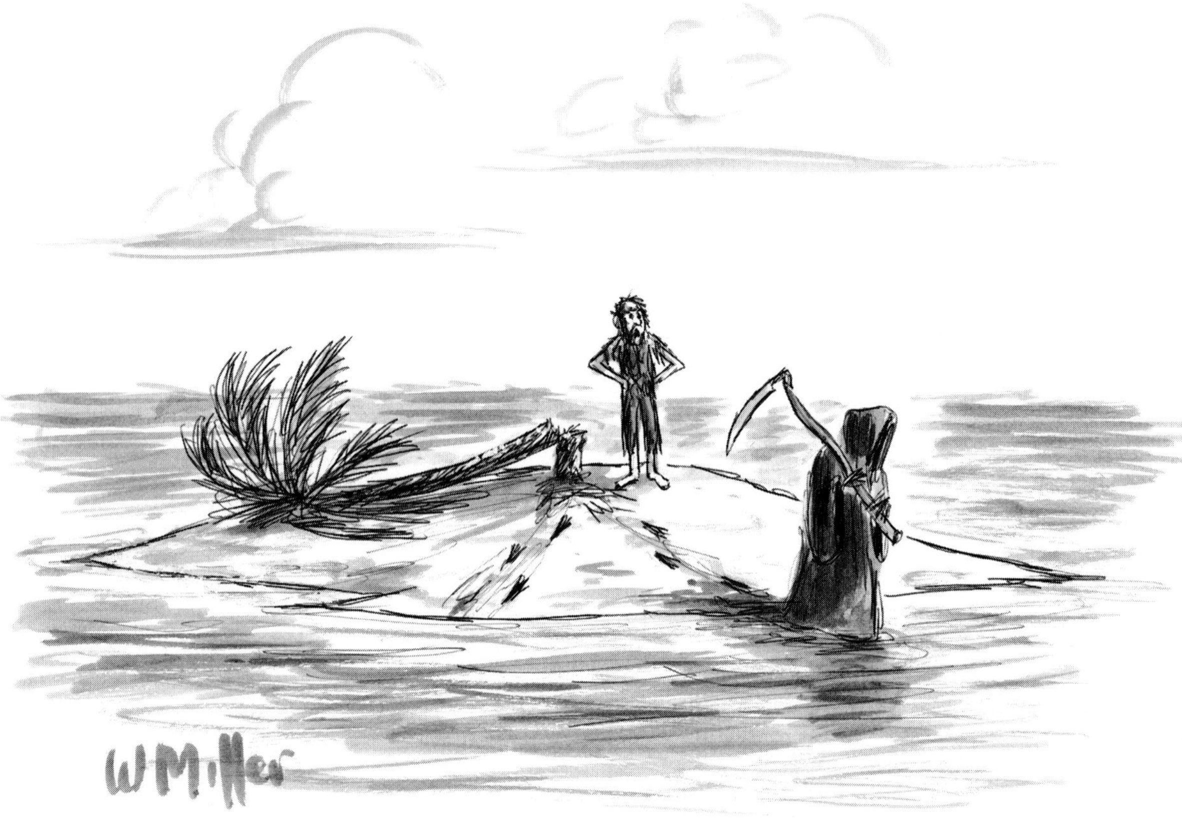
W Miller

"That's it?"

"This will lighten your mood, Dick—every few minutes, a baby boomer turns fifty."

"I should've made that sex tape."

"He never really lost his sense of humor. Did he?"

"Before I go over your test results, can we agree no one lives forever?"

"Hope you don't mind—it was his last request."

"Hi, I'm Death—more contemporary-looking than I used to be."

"All right, so there's been a mistake. Deal with it!"

"O.K., whose turn is it today to try and wrestle that plug away from Uncle Jim?"

"Uncertainty, Sylvia, is life's big draw."

"Actually, I preferred 'Heaven,' too, but then the marketing guys got hold of it."

"Isn't there a quicker way to kill me?"

"*Stanley, you son of a bitch, are you dead?*"

"He's one tough cookie. I've never seen anyone bounce back from an autopsy before."

"*This next tune is called 'Too Old to Party, but Too Young to Die.'*"

"Grandma's going to Florida."

"You had more money than God. That's a big no-no."

"Don't panic. I'm just a sore throat."

"And please join us after the service for the scattering of the deceased's ashes on
her mother's white carpeting."

"We'll have you out of here in no time."

"This is the first time I've heard a bagpipe play 'The Party's Over.'"

"Maynard, your deathbed confessions were <u>disgusting</u>! Do you hear me? <u>Disgusting!</u>"

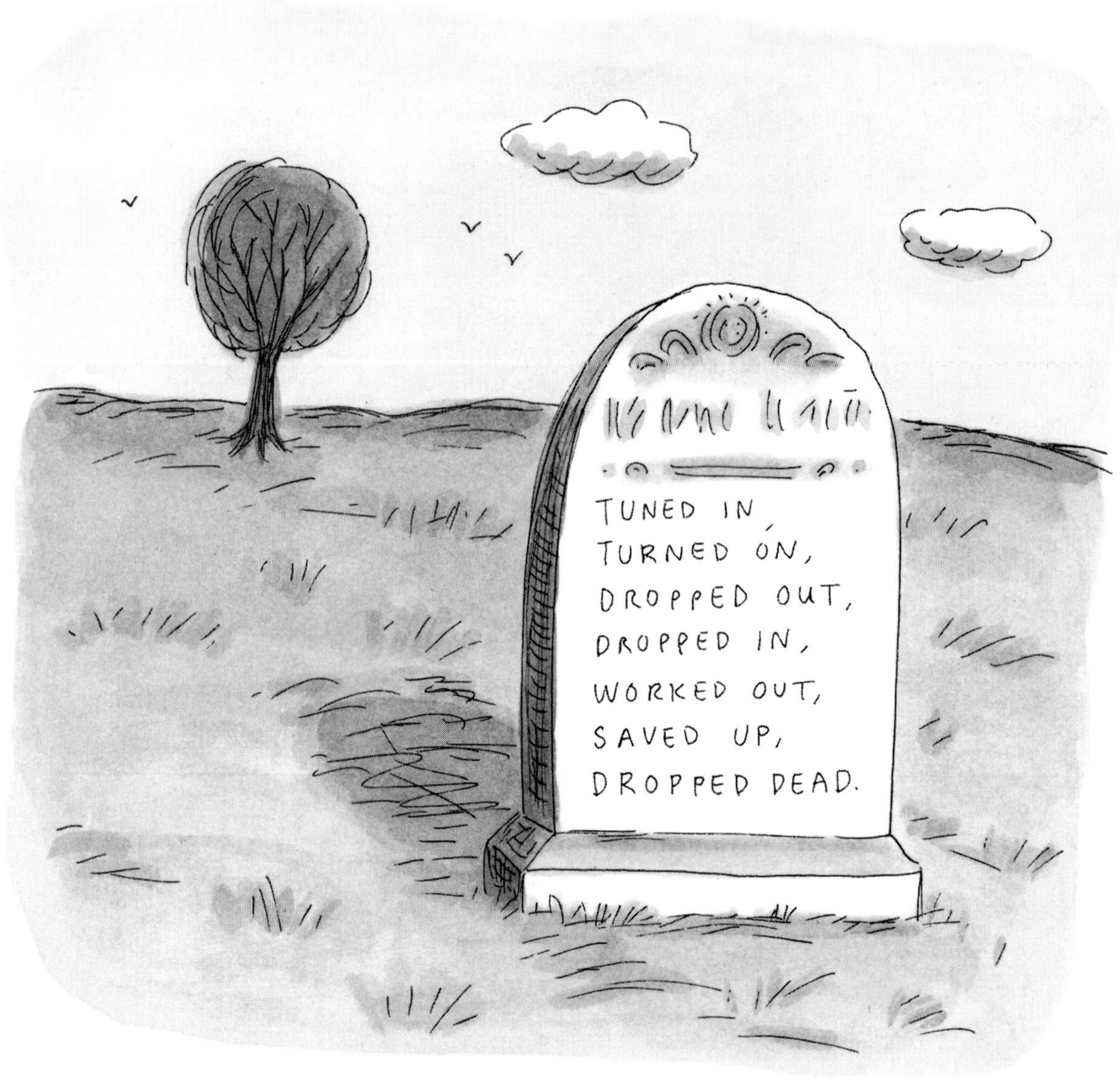
TUNED IN,
TURNED ON,
DROPPED OUT,
DROPPED IN,
WORKED OUT,
SAVED UP,
DROPPED DEAD.

"His favorite movie was 'Shane,' which he sat through twenty-seven times. Wow. This obituary really is thorough."

"It's the closure fairy."

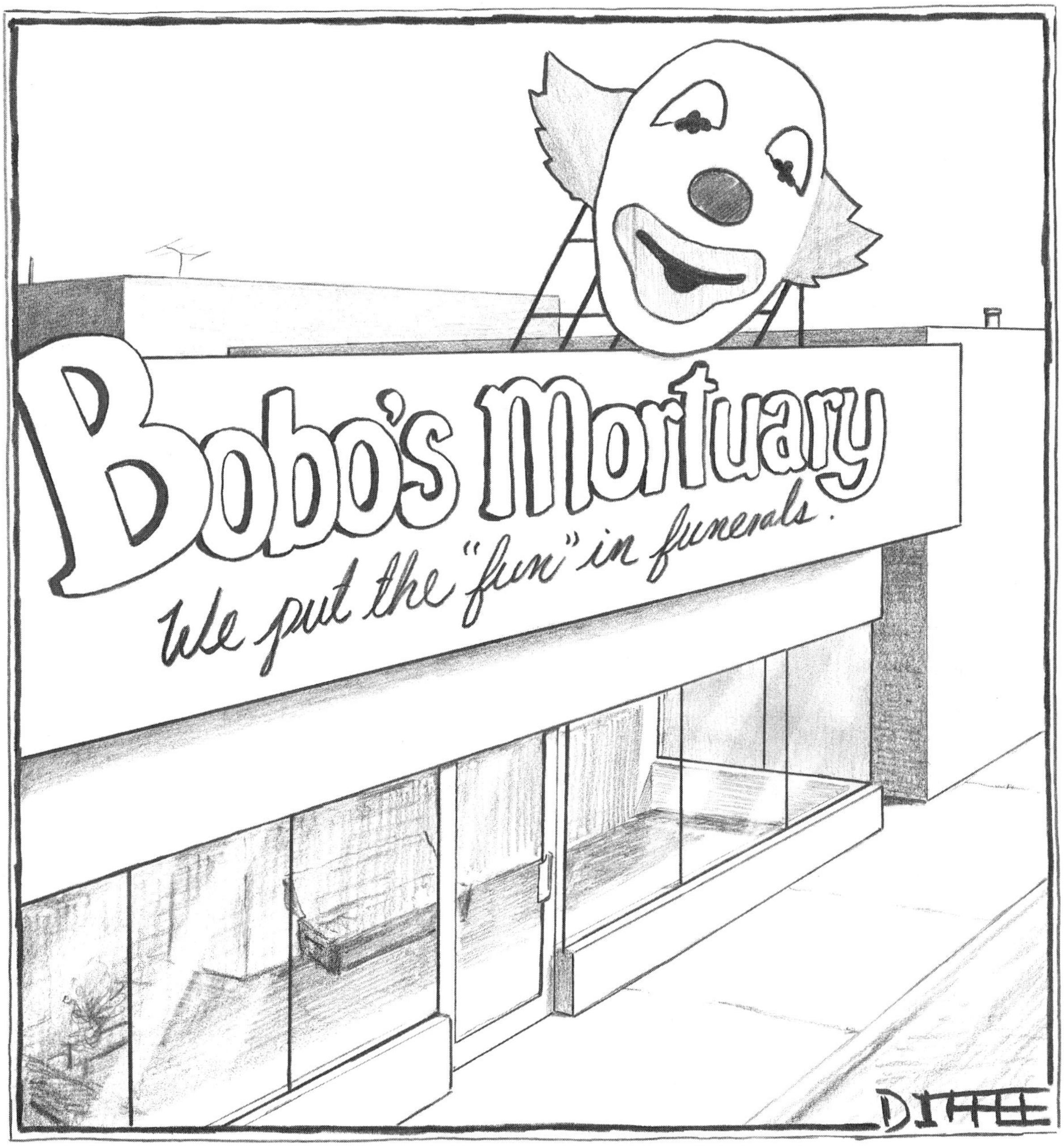
Bobo's Mortuary
We put the "fun" in funerals.
DIFFEE

"One last request: move my car to the 11:30 A.M. to 1 P.M. Monday–Thursday side of the street for tomorrow."

"When he pointed to his heart, I thought he was being romantic."

"Gracious me, I certainly never expected to run into you up here."

"... and don't forget to visit my new website: frank@thegreatbeyond.com."

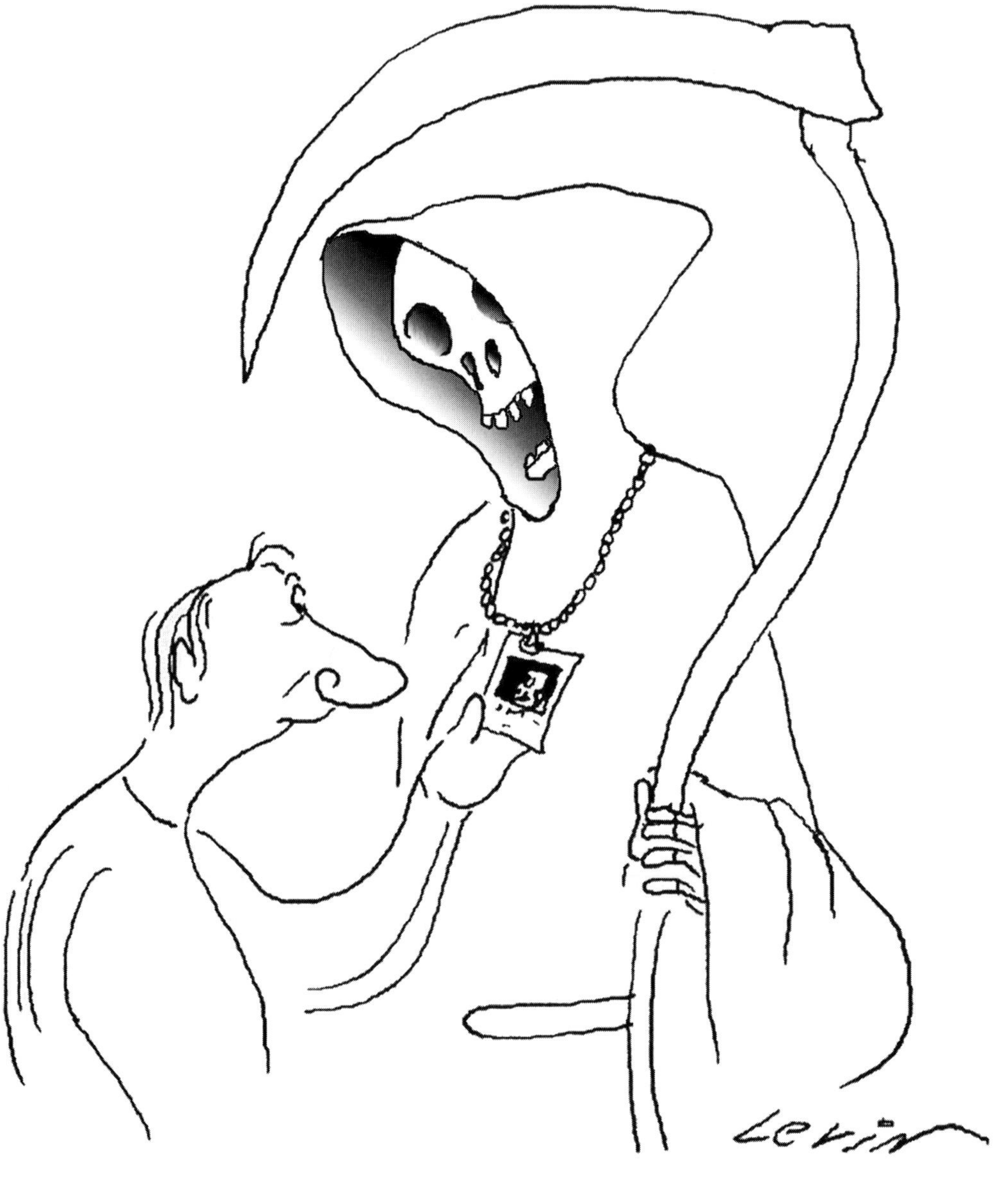
Levin

"Now may we go?"

CONTRIBUTORS

GEORGE BOOTH

BIO: George Booth.

1926 Cainsville, Mo.
6 a.m. Grandma's kitchen
(Baby had a sunk-in rib-cage)
Uncle "Ta Ta" said, "What's the matter with him?"
Dr. Duff said, "Some of them are like that.
He'll probably come out of it."

1930 Martinsville, Mo.
Neighbor Lady Broadbent said, "What's the matter with him?"

1944 Fairfax, Mo.
Agriculture Teacher Crawford; "What's the matter with him?"

1944 Parris Island
Drill Instructor Baird screamed, "What in hell is the matter with you?"

1946 Pearl Harbor
Company Commander Ford, "Reenlist?"

BOOTH'S PHOTO

1948 Chicago Academy of Fine Arts
Landlady Collins, "You can have the cot in the basement next to Arnett, Herndon, Harless, Palmer, the furness and Le Doux, dollar-fifty cents a week. Too much? What's the matter with you?"

1950 the Leatherneck Magazine, Wash. D.C.,
Sergeant Major, "You are late!"

1952 Collier's magazine, New York City
Secretary: "You can't just walk into Gurney Williams' office! What's the matter with you?"

1969 The New Yorker magazine
Secretary: "Come on in here! Mr. Geraghty is waiting! What's the matter with you?"

137

Q. When you were a kid what did you want to be when you grew up?

A. a cartoonist.

Q. What is the accomplishment of which you are most proud?

A. I snared Dione.

Q. What are your most current passions?

A. ① Cartooning ② Itchy ankles. ③ Gerberg

Q. List three things you haven't done, yet.

A. ① Haven't even started cartooning, yet.
② Haven't satisfied itchy ankles.
③ Haven't knocked Gerberg's head clean off, yet.

(Q.) What words of wisdom do you have?

(A.) Have a plan to git out of town when the bourgeoisie wiggles out the snaffle.

(Q.) How would you prefer to arrive at the end?

(A.) With a valid green card.

(Q.) Whom would you like to meet in the Great Beyond?

(A.) Gerberg.

(Q.) Sketch a scene from your funeral.

ROZ CHAST

I couldn't find a photo.

Roz Chast was born in Brooklyn, New York. Her cartoons frequently appear in *The New Yorker*. Her cartoons have also appeared in *Scientific American, The
Harvard Business Review, Mother Jones, Redbook,* and
many other magazines. Her most recent book is *Theories
of Everything: Selected, Collected, and Health-Inspected
Cartoons by Roz Chast, 1978–2006* (Bloomsbury).

1. When you were a kid, what did you want to be when you grew up?
   An artist.

2. What is the accomplishment of which you're most proud?
   My children.

3. List three things you haven't done yet.
   Eaten horseflesh
   Killed anyone
   Been to Mississippi

4. What are your most current passions?
   Knitting
   Gum

5. What words of wisdom do you have?
   Watch out for people who offer you words of wisdom.

6. How would you prefer to arrive at "The End"?
   Not in horrible, screaming pain.

7. Whom would you like to meet in The Great Beyond?
   My friends.

8. Imagine a scene from your funeral, and draw it.

I am tied to an inflatable raft and floated out to sea.

FRANK COTHAM

My childhood was uneventful, which I consider a pretty good thing, and I remember going to college and graduating with mediocre grades. Working for a TV station in Memphis was entertaining, especially the times when I was a courtroom illustrator. I'm no spring chicken—I've been drawing cartoons since the late seventies.

1. When you were a kid, what did you want to be when you grew up?

   I thought I would be what my father was—a sailor—but then he became a salesman and I became confused.

2. What is the accomplishment of which you're most proud?

   I'm very proud of my family, including my dog and cat family.

3. List three things you haven't done yet.

   I haven't made a huge fortune, and time is running out; I've never been to Europe; and I've never overcome my fear of boats and flying.

4. What are your most current passions?

   I enjoy photography, but I'm not very good at it, and I enjoy watching my wife watch basketball games—she's a hoot.

5. What words of wisdom do you have?

Be persistent, never give up, unless things are really hopeless—you should have the sense to know when that is.

6. How would you prefer to arrive at "The End"?

I don't want to have to deal with doctors, so I guess suddenly would be okay—and painlessly. But I wouldn't want to die at a sporting event where the fans just let you lie till the game's over.

7. Whom would you like to meet in The Great Beyond?

There is a certain grade-school-teacher art critic whom I would like to have a word with—she knows who she is.

8. Imagine a scene from your funeral, and draw it.

LEO CULLUM

I was born in Newark, New Jersey, in 1942. I graduated from Holy Cross College in 1963. In 1968 I joined TWA and flew for them for thirty-four years. I started at *The New Yorker* in 1973 mostly selling ideas to be redrawn by Charles Addams. My first drawing was published by *The New Yorker* in 1977. I'm married to Kathy and we have two daughters, Kimberly, twenty-five, and Kaitlin, twenty-one.

1. When you were a kid, what did you want to be when you grew up?
   Left-handed . . . and people could call me Lefty.

2. What is the accomplishment of which you're most proud?
   Serving in the Marine Corps in Vietnam.

3. List three things you haven't done yet.
   Cleaned out our garage
   Housebroken our cocker spaniel
   Eaten tofu

4. What are your most current passions?
   Painting . . . or rather, trying to start painting.

5. What words of wisdom do you have?
   Does it matter? Would anyone listen?

6. How would you prefer to arrive at "The End"?
   In comfy jammies.

7. Whom would you like to meet in The Great Beyond?
   ~~**Van Gogh, Cézanne, Monet**~~
   People who speak English.

8. Imagine a scene from your funeral, and draw it.

"IF YOU HURRY WE CAN MAKE HAPPY HOUR."

MATTHEW DIFFEE

I grew up in Denton, Texas, where thrice in my young life I was bitten by ponies. As a kid I spent a lot of time drawing. I also spent a lot of time throwing rocks at lizards, so I guess there was a point there where I could have gone either way. I'm not bragging—just saying. In college I majored in art and minored in creative writing, but I didn't think of putting the two together until I was twenty-nine years old. (By that time my dream of gathering together all the one-man bands of the world to form an International Super Orchestra had proved politically and logistically impossible.) I sold my first cartoon to *The New Yorker* pretty soon after that. Now I live in New York and hardly ever interact with ponies.

1. When you were a kid, what did you want to be when you grew up?
   Mexican.

2. What is the accomplishment of which you're most proud?
   I'm a joggling champion. If you don't know, joggling is a sport invented by jugglers in which you run and juggle at the same time. I placed first in the 400 meters in Buffalo a couple years ago. I'm pretty proud of that—also a little embarrassed.

3. List three things you haven't done yet.
   I've never karaoked, spelunked, or bivouacked.

4. What are your most current passions?
   Playing the banjo, playing the fiddle, playing the soccer, throwing rocks at lizards. I'm excited about designing mandolins with my high school buddy Ed McGee—I draw 'em, he builds 'em. I'm learning how to tie proper knots, and researching alternative energy sources to use in my dream shack that I plan to build soon. (Tidal energy—that's where it's at.) Oh, and I'm also getting really into making enchiladas. I'm tweaking various recipes until I create the perfect enchilada. I'm learning that enchiladas are like cartoons, you gotta make a bunch of bad ones before you can make any really good ones. On a good week I'll make as many as 120 enchiladas. I give a lot of them away.

5. What words of wisdom do you have?

Well, I think basically, you just gotta know when to hold 'em, know when to fold 'em, know when to walk away, and know when to run. You also probably shouldn't take your guns to town, and if there's any mothers reading this, do yourself and the rest of us a favor and don't let your babies grow up to be cowboys. Other than that just eat more vegetables, try to exercise.

6. How would you prefer to arrive at "The End"?

Sans vomit.

7. Whom would you like to meet in The Great Beyond?

The souls of hot babes.

8. Imagine a scene from your funeral, and draw it.

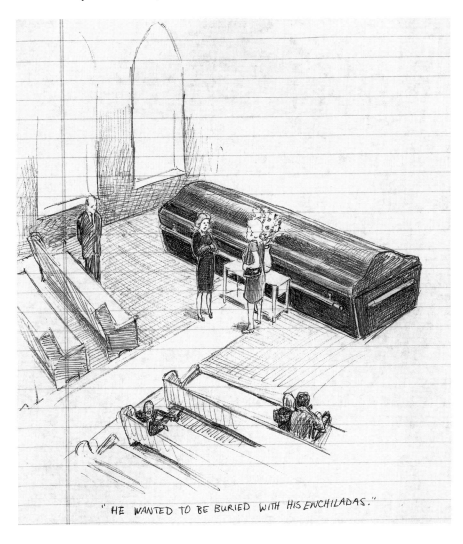

"HE WANTED TO BE BURIED WITH HIS ENCHILADAS."

MORT GERBERG

Mort Gerberg was born in Brooklyn, moved, then visited lots of other exotic places, such as India and Africa. He's published many magazine cartoons, mostly in *The New Yorker* and *Playboy,* comic strips, and edited, written, or illustrated forty books for adults and children, including his classic *Cartooning: The Art and the Business.* For other fun, he plays the piano, all sports, sings in a choir, and conducts Passover seders for thirty-plus people. He lives in Manhattan with his wife, Judith, with whom he parented their daughter, Lilia.

1. When you were a kid, what did you want to be when you grew up?
   Much taller, and the same age as all the other kids in my class.

2. What is the accomplishment of which you're most proud?
   a) Writing *Cartooning: The Art and the Business,* and feeling that it made a contribution.
   b) Playing on Harry Truman's piano in the U.S. State Department's Benjamin Franklin Room, in Washington, D.C.
   c) Playing second base for *The New Yorker* softball team.

3. List three things you haven't done yet.
   a) Skied a double-black-diamond mogul glade trail at Vail, say.
   b) Had my head examined for *thinking* about skiing a double-black-diamond mogul glade trail at Vail, say.
   c) Paid a visit to The Great Beyond.
   d) Written the great-American-short-Jewish-kid-from-Brooklyn-with-glasses-who-moved-to-Manhattan-and-made-good-more-or-less novel.

4. What are your most current passions?
   a) Clearing out my files and getting rid of all that stuff.
   b) Hitting my topspin backhand more, instead of the slice.
   c) Whatever is on my drawing board or in my notebook right now.
   d) Getting people to differentiate correctly between *it's* and *its, less* and *fewer, their* and *they're,* and to stop using plural pronouns to refer to singular nouns.

5. What words of wisdom do you have?
   a) Listen to what your stomach tells you.
   b) Redo it one more time.
   c) Always run for the bus.

6. How would you prefer to arrive at "The End"?
   With all my major parts in fine working order, especially my brain. (See the introduction.) And from that spot, I'd like a stretch limo stocked with authentic chocolate egg creams and a driver who doesn't yak on his cell phone.

7. Whom would you like to meet in The Great Beyond?
   Gloria Silver from first grade, who looked at me in a way I didn't understand. And Moses, to find out a few things—you know, from the horse's mouth. All my loved ones, of course. And maybe some unloved ones, for a different reason. Also Art Tatum, so I could see him play what my ears told me was impossible.

8. Imagine a scene from your funeral, and draw it.

SAM GROSS

SAM GROSS WAS BORN IN THE BRONX WAY BEFORE HIP-HOP WAS BORN THERE. HE HAS BEEN DRAWING CARTOONS FOR 45 YEARS SO HE KNOWS WHAT IT'S LIKE TO BE OLD AND FORGETFUL. THERE ARE OVER 24,700 CARTOONS IN HIS GAG FILE AND HE ONLY REMEMBERS SOME OF THEM.

1. When you were a kid, what did you want to be when you grew up?

   A VERY OLD CARTOONIST.

2. What is the accomplishment of which you're most proud?

   BEING AROUND LONG ENOUGH TO HAVE A CHANCE AT BEING A VERY OLD CARTOONIST.

3. List three things you haven't done yet.

   MADE AN INSANE AMOUNT OF MONEY.
   LOST MY MARBLES.
   RUN OFF WITH THE HOME HEALTH AIDE.

4. What are your most current passions?

   THE HOME HEALTH AIDE. HER NAME IS YOLANDA.

5. What words of wisdom do you have?

HAVE THE HOME HEALTH AIDE CHECKED OUT FOR SOCIAL DISEASES.

6. How would you prefer to arrive at "The End"?

VERTICAL AND CAPABLE OF CHANGING MY MIND.

7. Whom would you like to meet in The Great Beyond?

MARVIN PORTNOY. HE OWES ME MONEY.

8. Imagine a scene from your funeral, and draw it.

J. B. HANDELSMAN

BIO

Born in New York City; lived there until drafted into the U.S. Army in World War II. Won the war, with a little help. Studied electrical engineering under the G.I. bill, but gave it up to do what is now called graphic design. Dissatisfied with that as well, turned to cartooning. Moved to England with family and was there for 18 years. Married, three children, God knows how many grandchildren.

ANSWERS TO EIGHT QUESTIONS

1. When I was a kid, I wanted to be a toymaker (inspired by the operetta "Babes in Toyland").

2. I am most proud of a series I did weekly for 11 years for Punch, called Freaky Fables.

3. Three things I haven't done yet: 1. Murdered an editor.
                                    2. Been elected president.
                                    3. Fought Muhammad Ali.

4. My current passions are fame, money, and women.

5. Words of wisdom: Don't say things you will regret -- especially to people who would take offense and try to ruin you.

6. If I really have to die, and I don't see why I should, it would preferably be in my sleep. Then again, perhaps not. Just don't let it be too painful.

7. I'd like to meet my parents and ask them some hard questions to which, of course, I know the answers.

8. I'd rather not. Sorry.

SIDNEY HARRIS

In my youth, during WWII, I was held prisoner five days a wk. at PS 177 in B'klyn. Later I went to JHS 228. In those days children were allowed to ride the subways—I used mainly the BMT and IRT, rarely the IND—unaccompanied, and I traveled far and wide within NYC. Thus I became very much at home with abbreviations. It's a brief step from there to drawing cartoons, which are abbr. pieces of fict.

1. When you were a kid, what did you want to be when you grew up?

   Alas, Duke Snider was playing center field for the Dodgers, and I realized I could never be six feet two inches tall and two hundred pounds. Or hit a curveball.

2. What is the accomplishment of which you're most proud?

   This is hypothetical, but if I won the Nobel Prize for something, I'd really show off.

3. List three things you haven't done yet.

   1. Learned to play the piano like Art Tatum.
   2. Learned to play the piano like Bud Powell.
   3. Learned to play the piano like Lennie Tristano.

4. What are your most current passions?

   Baseball—the statistics, not all that running around.
   Music—the notes, not all that noise.
   Art—the ink . . . you get it.

5. What words of wisdom do you have?

   A square plus B square doesn't have to equal C square. I'm working on it.

6. How would you prefer to arrive at "The End"?

   So out of touch, I had no idea what was going on. Wait—that was yesterday.

7. Whom would you like to meet in The Great Beyond?

Adam—to see if that story about him is true.

8. Imagine a scene from your funeral, and draw it.

ED KOREN

30 MARCH 07

MORT —
HERE ARE THE RESPONSES TO QUESTIONS
POSED

BIO
ED KOREN GREW UP IN MT. VERNON, N.Y. —
THE VERY SAME SUBURB WHICH HOSTED THE
EARLY LIFE OF ONE OF HIS INSPIRATIONAL
FIGURES — E.B. WHITE. COLUMBIA COLLEGE,
ATELIER 17 (PARIS) AND PRATT INSTITUTE WERE
HIS FORMAL EDUCATORS. HE HAS CONTRIBUTED
TO THE NEW YORKER FOR 45 YEARS, AS WELL
AS AN ARRAY OF PUBLICATIONS AND PUBLISHERS.
HE CONTINUES TO WORK OBSESSIVLY ON CARTOONS,
ILLUSTRATIONS, BOOKS, PRINTS AND DRAWINGS.

ANSWERS TO QUESTIONS

1. I WAS NEVER SURE UNTIL I SORT OF FELL BY A SERIES OF SERENDIPITOUS EVENTS, INTO WHAT I HAVE NOW DONE FOR A LIFETIME.

2. A LIFE'S WORTH OF KIDS, FAMILY, FRIENDS; A SATISFYING BODY OF WORK; AND A SENSE OF HAVING BEEN OF SERVICE, IN MANY DIFFERENT WAYS — AND PARTICULARLY (AS A MEMBER OF THE FIRE SERVICE) HELPING MITIGATE THE CHANCE DISASTERS IN MY SMALL COMMUNITY.

3. LIKE THE GREAT JAPANESE MASTER HOKUSAI, UNDERSTAND THE NATURE OF THINGS (LIFE, ART, PRETTY MUCH EVERYTHING).

4. CONTINUING STUDY, CONTINUING CURIOSITY, CONTINUING ALERTNESS TO THE TELLINGLY SMALL, REVEALING MOMENTS THAT SERENDIPITOUSLY SWIM BY MY VIEW.

5. WHATEVER ONE IS DOING, BE A WORLD-CLASS NOTICER.

6. AFTER A DENSE AND LUMINOUS SNOWFALL — WITH THE SUN AT FULL BORE — IN THE MIXED FOREST OR ON THE BROW OF A HILL AND ON MY GREASED CROSS-COUNTRY SKIS OR MY PRIZED BICYCLE, OR ON A SPECTACULAR BODY OF WATER IN MY SLEEK KAYAK.

7. ALL THE WRITERS, ARTISTS, MUSICIANS, ETC. — WHOSE WORK AND VOICES I HAVE REVERED AND WHOSE EXPERIENCE HAS DEEPENED MINE.

(8) SURE ATTACHING

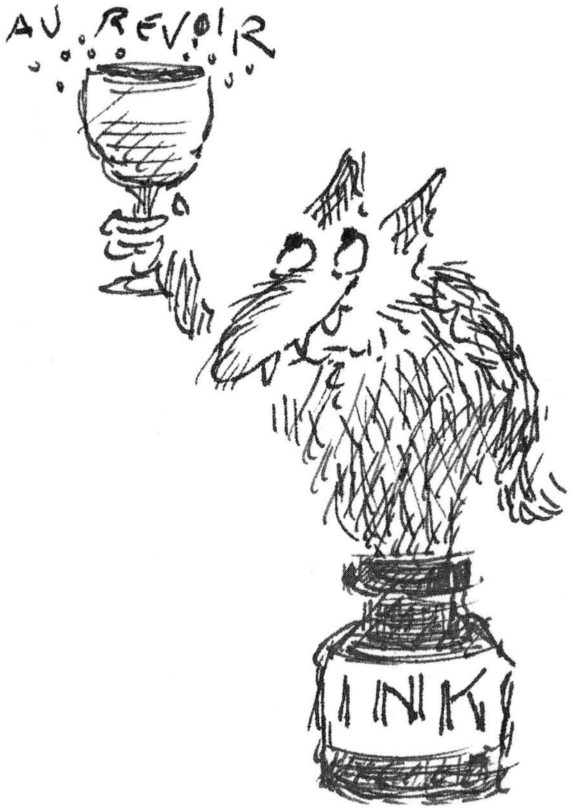
AU REVOIR
INK

GLEN LE LIEVRE

Glen Le Lievre lives in a fort made from sofa cushions somewhere in New York City. He has drawn cartoons for *MAD*, *Playboy*, and *The New Yorker* partly for the money, but mostly because it annoys the crap out of his in-laws. While not religious, he believes that in the afterlife there is a mint on every pillow.

1. When you were a kid, what did you want to be when you grew up?

A SKIN DIVER —OR A TRUCK.

2. What is the accomplishment of which you're most proud?

NOT BECOMING A TRUCK.

3. List three things you haven't done yet.

FILLED UP WITH DIESEL.
CHASED DENNIS WEAVER ACROSS THE CALIFORNIA DESERT.
CARRIED A HALF-TON OF GRAVEL ON MY BACK.

4. What are your most current passions?

LICKING BATTERIES.
TOUCHING THE THIRD RAIL.
SHOWERING WITH MY TOASTER.

5. What words of wisdom do you have?

SAPIENCE, SOUNDNESS, SAGACIOUSNESS, PROFUNDITY.

6. How would you prefer to arrive at "The End"?

IN MY SEAT HOLDING AN EMPTY POPCORN BUCKET.

7. Whom would you like to meet in The Great Beyond?

A DAZZLING VARIETY OF MULTI-COLORED FISH, OTHER DIVERS...
WAIT, WE ARE TALKING ABOUT THE GREAT BARRIER REEF, AREN'T WE?

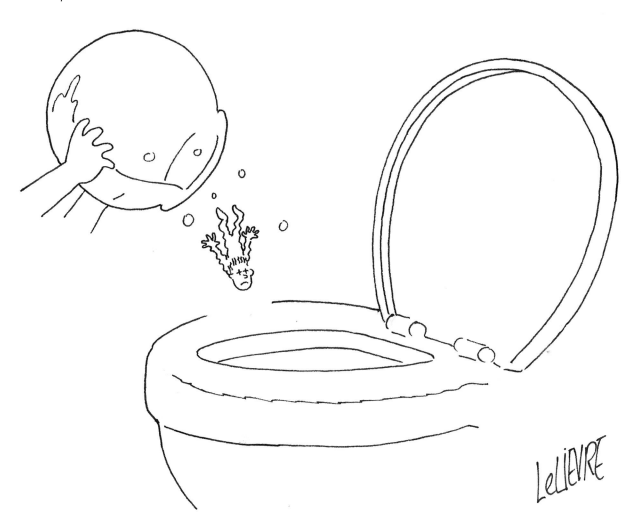

ARNIE LEVIN

Born 2/11/38, in Brooklyn, NY . . . Moved to Miami, Florida (accompanied by parents) . . . Graduated Miami Technical High School, June 1955 . . . USMC, 1955–1958 . . . Returned to New York, 1958 . . . Art Students League 1958/59 . . . Partner, Seven Arts Coffee Shop, 1959–1964.

Bummed around 1964–1967 . . . School of Visual Arts/Blechman-Slackman Class (evenings) . . . Messenger, Push Pin Studio, 1967 . . . Animation director/designer, Electra Studio, 1968–1972 . . . Freelance animation, Pablo Ferro, Stars and Stripes . . . Partner, Phos-Cine Production, Animated Motion Picture Studio, 1974 . . . *New Yorker*, 1974– . . . Taught at Pratt, CW Post, New School, Parsons, Adelphi. Currently teaching at School of Visual Arts . . .

1. When you were a kid, what did you want to be when you grew up?
   I wanted to be not grown-up.

2. What is the accomplishment of which you're most proud?
   Surviving the system.

3. List three things you haven't done yet.
   1: Being able to draw a bowling pin symmetrically
   2: Spelling *Wedenesday* without using spell-check
   3: Finding two black socks that match

4. What are your most current passions?
   Enjoying life
   Enjoying work
   Enjoying people

5. What words of wisdom do you have?
   Do everything with passion, abandonment, and love . . .
   Appreciate and respect your gifts . . .

6. How would you prefer to arrive at "The End"?
You Cry When You're Born, So Rejoice When You Die . . .

7. Whom would you like to meet in The Great Beyond?
Everyone . . .

8. Imagine a scene from your funeral, and draw it.

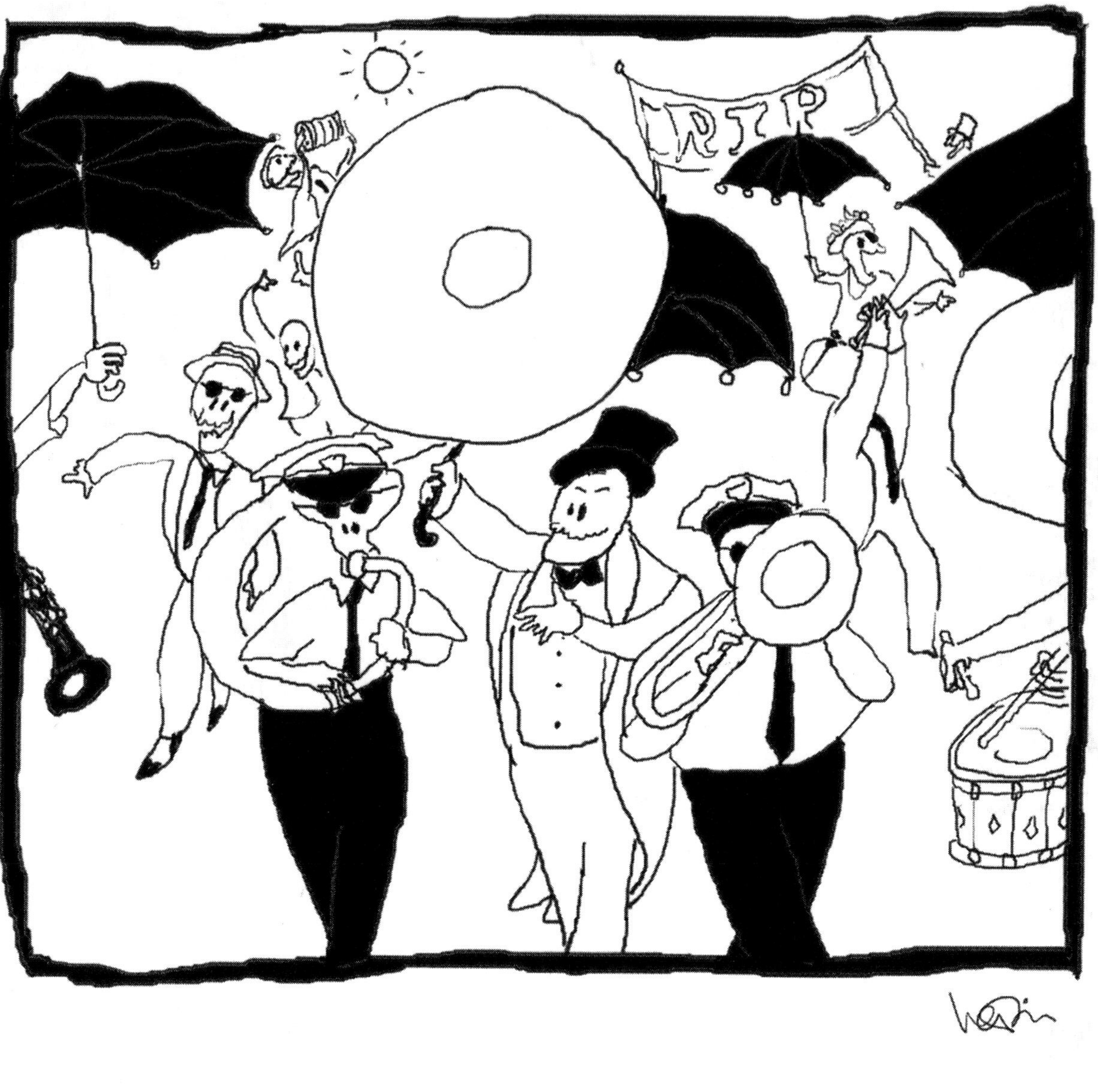
RIP

LEE LORENZ

- Born in 1932 in Hackensack, New Jersey.
- Grew up loving Milton Caniff, Disney, and later, Steinberg, but never planned to be a cartoonist.
- Studied at Carnegie Tech (now called Carnegie Mellon) and Pratt Institute.
- To support growing family began cartooning in 1955. Joined *The New Yorker* in 1958. Art editor there from 1973 to 1997.
- Three marriages, three children, and two grandchildren.
- Plays jazz cornet as a vocation.

1. When you were a kid, what did you want to be when you grew up?
   A "scientific invention" (inspired by my favorite radio serial, *Lorenzo Jones and His Wife Belle*).

2. What is the accomplishment of which you're most proud?
   Bringing a new generation of cartoonists to *The New Yorker*.

3. List three things you haven't done yet.
   Skydiving, spelunking, cross-channel swimming.

4. What are your most current passions?
   Wellbutrin, clonazepam, Lipitor.

5. What words of wisdom do you have?
   Only steal from the best.

6. How would you prefer to arrive at "The End"?
   In a sealed railroad car with all the people I hate.

7. Whom would you like to meet in The Great Beyond?
   Nikola Tesla (no kidding!).

8. Imagine a scene from your funeral, and draw it.

MARISA ACOCELLA MARCHETTO

Marisa has done a ton of cartoons for a lot of great magazines and was the first cartoonist ever to have an ongoing comic in *The New York Times*. She is the author of two graphic memoirs, one of which, *Cancer Vixen,* is about how she sketched herself kicking cancer's butt, had that image in her head for the entire year she received treatment for breast cancer, and feels that in a weird way she literally drew herself healthy.

1. When you were a kid, what did you want to be when you grew up?
   Buff, like Mort Gerberg. Actually, a shooting guard for the New York Knicks. But now I've given up my hoop addiction and am obsessed with baseball.

2. What is the accomplishment of which you're most proud?
   Laughing in the face of cancer, and drawing myself healthy, literally.

3. List three things you haven't done yet.
   1. Win the Nobel Prize. 2. Win an Academy Award. 3. Go to the dentist.

4. What are your most current passions?
   Finishing these questions.

5. What words of wisdom do you have?

Live your life and don't spend time thinking about words of wisdom.

6. How would you prefer to arrive at "The End"?

At peace.

7. Whom would you like to meet in The Great Beyond?

Gianni Versace, and have him suit me up for an eternity. Actually, Jesus would be kind of cool, and I'm a big fan of his mother. Also, I'd like to ask Nostradamus to decode those silly quatrains.

8. Imagine a scene from your funeral, and draw it.

ABSOLUTELY NOT!!!!!! Whatever you draw, you draw to you. I'm living proof of that.

WARREN MILLER

Warren Miller
Born in Chicago.
Moved to New York in 1961.
Cartoons have appeared in
various publications but
mostly in The New Yorker.
Also paints on canvas
using colors squeezed from
tubes.
Still lives in New York City
with wife. Has three grown
children and one grandchild.

1. When you were a kid, what did you want to be when you grew up?

A motorman on the Chicago, North Shore,
and Milwaukee electric railway

2. What is the accomplishment of which you're most proud?

Luckily, I never became a motorman.
- The Chicago, North Shore, and Milwaukee
went out of business in the early 1960's.

3. **List three** things you haven't done yet.

Ice skated, Roller skated,
or joined a circus.

4. What are your most current passions?

Trying to wake up in the morning
with a good attitude.

5. What words of wisdom do you have?

A fish tank can be a magnet for wealth and prosperity. The fish symbolize never-ending abundance.

6. How would you prefer to arrive at "The End"?

Nicely asleep

7. Whom would you like to meet in The Great Beyond?

OLd UNFATHOMABLE

8. Imagine a scene from your funeral, and draw it.

8. MY FUNERAL

ASSORTED MOURNERS

RADIO-CONTROLLED TOY BULLDOZER

MY ASHES

MY FINAL RESTING PLACE

WMiller

FRANK MODELL

Frank Modell says he doesn't do questionnaires, but after taking a glance at the questions, he handed me this:
—M.G.

I grew up in Philadelphia, where my earliest memory was of wanting to be a street cleaner. I liked the starched white uniforms and their big bristled brushes. I liked the sounds they made swishing slush down the gutters of our small Philly street. No doubt why today I aspire to be well tailored and paint with fine expensive brushes.

I graduated from the Pennsylvania Museum School of Art and was drafted into the army immediately after that. I then spent four and a half years in Europe with World War Two, where I came out as a first sergeant. At the same time began contributing cartoon ideas to *The New Yorker*, drew cartoons for them, and became part of the art department. All this way back when Harold Ross was the editor.

Have strong wannabe urges and tried short-story writing, playwriting, stand-up, acting, poetry, inventing, and tap dancing to name a few.

I have no expectations for a postdeath social life. For me it's simply lights out and good-bye, Charlie. I am torn between a need to be reclusive and a need to be gregarious. Sometimes both at the same time. I try living with passion, staying proactive, staying disciplined, and being grateful.

A life of drawing funny pictures for a living is as good as it gets.

VICTORIA ROBERTS

Victoria Roberts has worked as a cartoonist for *The New Yorker* since 1988. Her work also appears regularly in *The New York Times* and *The Australian*. Ms. Roberts has written and illustrated twenty books, including *Cattitudes, Is Your Cat Gay?* and *Is Your Dog Gay?* and *Halloweena*.

1. When you were a kid, what did you want to be when you grew up?
   I wanted to be in the theater. I was a child actor for a bit.

2. What is the accomplishment of which you're most proud?
   Getting into *The New Yorker* and creating a character, Nona Appleby, onstage.

3. List three things you haven't done yet.
   Traveled to Rajasthan, Angkor Wat, or Machu Picchu.

4. What are your most current passions?
   Working with my stage character Nona Appleby.

5. What words of wisdom do you have?
   None. (This is the wisest I have ever been!)

6. How would you prefer to arrive at "The End"?
   Softly and with all of my faculties, and well loved.

7. Whom would you like to meet in The Great Beyond?
   Probably the people I love in the here and now, as well as some I have loved and lost. And Bill Robinson if he's available for private coaching.

8. Imagine a scene from your funeral, and draw it.

This is me at Frank Campbell's on Madison.
The pug has dropped by an excellent
butcher shop nearby, Lobel's.

DAVID SIPRESS

David Sipress has published over three hundred cartoons in *The New Yorker* since 1998. His work has appeared pretty much everywhere else. He has authored eight books of cartoons and illustrated numerous others. He is the writer, producer, and host of *Conversations with Cartoonists,* an ongoing series of performances featuring cartoon-based humor and interviews with great *New Yorker* cartoonists. He lives in Brooklyn with his wife, Ginny.

1. When you were a kid, what did you want to be when you grew up?
   Who said I wanted to grow up? A cartoonist, of course.

2. What is the accomplishment of which you're most proud?
   Growing up.

3. List three things you haven't done yet.
   Calmed down. Read Proust. Died.

4. What are your most current passions?
   Omigod—I don't have any! Do you think that's a problem? Great! Now I've got something else to worry about. Wait a second—what about worrying? Is worrying a passion?

5. What words of wisdom do you have?
   Be rich, successful, and good-looking.

6. How would you prefer to arrive at "The End"?
   Late.

7. Whom would you like to meet in The Great Beyond?
   A young Brigitte Bardot. Two young Brigitte Bardots.

8. Imagine a scene from your funeral, and draw it.

He has risen!

BARBARA SMALLER

Barbara Smaller grew up outside Chicago. She attended many different and sundry universities. Ditto, jobs. She lived as a drifter and a grifter . . . Actually just as a drifter. Gradually her cartoons appeared in publications; and then in 1996, suddenly, without warning, regularly in *The New Yorker*. According to Wikipedia, she currently lives in NYC with her husband and daughter.

1. When you were a kid, what did you want to be when you grew up?

   An international secret agent or something that could Fly

2. What is the accomplishment of which you're most proud?

   being cast as Esther in the sixth grade Purim operetta, I peaked early

3. List three things you haven't done yet.

   been tall, been rich, been blonde

4. What are your most current passions?

   napping and national health insurance

5. What words of wisdom do you have?

none, no···none at all·· maybe words of idiocy

6. How would you prefer to arrive at "The End"?

I would like all my body parts to go more or less at the same time.

7. Whom would you like to meet in The Great Beyond?

I know who I wouldn't want to meet; people I owe money to and pretty much anybody from high school.

8. Imagine a scene from your funeral, and draw it.

my ashes in a nice jelly jar

MICK STEVENS

Between heroic acts I have found ample time to pursue other interests and vocations, among them magazine cartooning. My work has appeared in many magazines over the years (only to mysteriously disappear in the next issue, a process I never fully understood). Luckily for me, one of the magazines that has accepted my work has been *The New Yorker*, for which I'm eternally grateful.

1. When you were a kid, what did you want to be when you grew up?
   A superhero. I didn't particularly care for the outfits, though. Maybe a Clark Kent who didn't have to changes clothes when saving people.

2. What is the accomplishment of which you're most proud?
   Deflecting a huge meteorite that threatened to collide with Earth in 1993. I've never mentioned it until now.
      You're welcome.

3. List three things you haven't done yet.
   1. Fried an egg without breaking the yolk.
   2. Had my name used in the *New York Times* Sunday crossword.
   3. Given a straight answer in a questionnaire.

4. What are your most current passions?
   I never got over my crush on Veronica Lake in *Sullivan's Travels*, God help me.

5. What words of wisdom do you have?

I'm still waiting for that big box of Wisdom that is supposed to come to people when they get older. So far it hasn't arrived. I should probably give the UPS people a call.

6. How would you prefer to arrive at "The End"?

Fashionably late.

7. Whom would you like to meet in The Great Beyond?

Someone in the accounting department.

8. Imagine a scene from your funeral, and draw it.

"It was in his will. He wanted to be late for his own funeral."

MIKE TWOHY

Mike Twohy intended to paint and teach art after receiving an MFA degree from the University of California at Berkeley, but he was seduced by cartooning in the late seventies and has been freelancing ever since. He is the creator of the syndicated panel *That's Life* and is a regular contributor to *The New Yorker*. He lives with his wife and two children near San Francisco.

1. When you were a kid, what did you want to be when you grew up?
   A clown, Robin Hood, or a cartoonist

2. What is the accomplishment of which you're most proud?
   Recorded my a cappella cover of the Beach Boys' *Sounds of Summer*

3. List three things you haven't done yet.
   Checked e-mail
   Learned "Happy Birthday" on the piano
   Released my a cappella cover of the Beach Boys' *Sounds of Summer*

4. What are your most current passions?
   Looking incredulous
   Filling the bird feeder

5. What words of wisdom do you have?
   Never force your assistant to fill out personal questionnaires for you!

6. How would you prefer to arrive at "The End"?
   Wearing pants

7. Whom would you like to meet in The Great Beyond?
   God

8. Imagine a scene from your funeral, and draw it.

P. C. VEY

P. C. Vey is a cartoonist and humorous illustrator who resides in New York with his wife, Tina, and cat, Otto, who may someday be documented as the world's oldest cat.

He is a regular contributor to *The New Yorker, Harvard Business Review, Barron's, MAD, The Boston Globe, The Wall Street Journal,* and *The New York Times.*

1. When you were a kid, what did you want to be when you grew up?

    WELL HIDDEN

2. What is the accomplishment of which you're most proud?

    LIVING UNDER AN ASSUMED NAME.

3. List three things you haven't done yet.

    BREATHE EASILY
    SLEEP SOUNDLY
    FIND AFFORDABLE LUXURY

4. What are your most current passions?

    TRYING TO BREATHE EASILY
    TRYING TO SLEEP SOUNDLY
    TRYING TO FIND AFFORDABLE LUXURY

5. What words of wisdom do you have?

LEAVE BEFORE IT'S TOO LATE.

6. How would you prefer to arrive at "The End"?

OUT OF BREATH.

7. Whom would you like to meet in The Great Beyond?

SOMEONE I HAVEN'T MET.

8. Imagine a scene from your funeral, and draw it.

KIM WARP

Kim Warp lives in Virginia Beach, Virginia, with her husband, two daughters, three cats, and a recently acquired dog the cats have convinced is an inferior cat. Her cartoons appear in *The New Yorker*, *Barron's*, and other magazines. When not cartooning or thinking about cartooning, she spends her time going to the beach, looking in the mailbox for checks, and admiring the palm tree in the backyard.

1. When you were a kid, what did you want to be when you grew up?

    A fighter pilot, a scientist, and a cartoonist.

2. What is the accomplishment of which you're most proud?

    When I was about two, I could only draw legs by drawing a box and then drawing a line down the middle. I still remember the thrill of learning how to draw separate legs.

3. List three things you haven't done yet.

    Become a fighter pilot, a scientist, or gotten all the laundry done at once.

4. What are your most current passions?

    Pens, pens, pens!

5. What words of wisdom do you have?

    Don't do the laundry, see what happens!

6. How would you prefer to arrive at "The End"?

Unexpectedly.

7. Whom would you like to meet in The Great Beyond?

Abraham Lincoln. I'm guessing his funniest anecdotes didn't make it into the history books.

8. Imagine a scene from your funeral, and draw it.

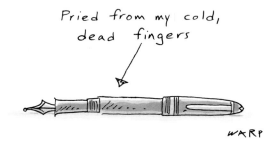

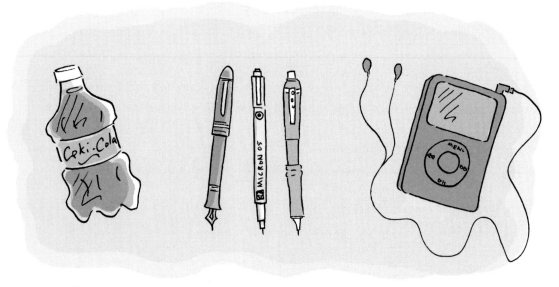

ROBERT WEBER

BIO

BORN AND RAISED
IN LOS ANGELES.
THAT'S IT.

1. When you were a kid, what did you want to be when you grew up?

TALLER

2. What is the accomplishment of which you're most proud?

BREATHING

3. List three things you haven't done yet.

1. VOTED REPUBLICAN.
2. FALLEN OUT OF BED.
3. TURNED DOWN A GLASS OF CHAMPAGNE.

4. What are your most current passions?

WOMEN
STAYING ALIVE

5. What words of wisdom do you have?

GET A JOB

6. How would you prefer to arrive at "The End"?

TAKE A SHARP RIGHT TURN AND KEEP GOING,

7. Whom would you like to meet in The Great Beyond?

MY COUSIN RICHARD — HE OWES ME,

8. Imagine a scene from your funeral, and draw it.

GAHAN WILSON

Bio.
    So far, so good.

1. To become a cartoonist.
2. To actually have become a cartoonist.
3. I haven't thought up a serious answer to your question.
   I haven't thought up an amusing answer to your question.
   I haven't answered your question.
4. Being sufficiently grateful for what has inspired those passions.
5. Far fewer than I used to have.
6. So abruptly and unexpectedly that I miss experiencing the whole thing.
7. I expect to meet nobody nor anything in the Great Beyond including The Great Beyond.
8. Since I have no desire to have a funeral held for me I hope it looks something like the following blank space.

JACK ZIEGLER

BRIEF BIO

BORN NEW YORK CITY, 1942. B.A., FORDHAM UNIVERSITY, 1964. FREELANCE CARTOONIST SINCE 1972. UNDER CONTRACT WITH THE NEW YORKER SINCE 1974. HAVE HAD NINE COLLECTIONS OF DRAWINGS PUBLISHED SINCE 1978 — PLUS ONE CHILDREN'S BOOK IN 1993.

1. When you were a kid what did you want to be when you grew up?
   TAX-FREE.

2. What is the accomplishment of which you're most proud?
   BREAKING INTO, AND BECOMING A REGULAR, AT THE NEW YORKER MAGAZINE.

3. List three things you haven't done yet.
   EATEN CHOCOLATE-COATED ANTS;
   LOST MY MIND;
   GONE TO MARS.

4. What are your most current passions?
   GETTING THE IDIOT BUSH AND ALL OF HIS ILK OUT OF OFFICE.

5. What words of wisdom do you have?
   DON'T TUG ON SUPERMAN'S CAPE;
   DON'T SPIT INTO THE WIND;
   DON'T PULL THE MASK OFF THE OLD LONE RANGER;
   AND (ABOVE ALL) DON'T MESS AROUND WITH JIM.

6. How would you prefer to arrive at "The End"?

BEING ZAPPED OUT OF EXISTENCE BY A GIGANTIC, RAYGUN-TOTING MONSTER FROM OUTER SPACE. THAT WOULD BE TOTALLY COOL.

7. Whom would you like to meet in The Great Beyond?

HENRY MILLER, RIN TIN TIN (THE ORIGINAL ONE, NOT ONE OF THOSE FAKE LATER ONES).

8. Imagine a scene from your funeral, and draw it.

NO FUNERAL — JUST ME IN A HEFTY BAG WAITING FOR PICK-UP OUT AT THE CURB.

ACKNOWLEDGMENTS

To start with, I acknowledge my gene pool, which is the main reason I'm still around making waves, and its foremost representative, Dr. I. J. Flance, aka my ninety-six-year-old uncle Jerry, a quintessential role model, not only for me and my family, but for the city of St. Louis, and beyond.

My agent, David Kuhn, wins my great appreciation for his publishing acumen and creativity, and for his laserlike guidance, with Billy Kingsland, in helping transform my original idea into an exciting reality.

I am very grateful to my editor, Nan Graham, who, along with Anna deVries, immediately knew what I was aiming for in this collection, kept raising its bar of excellence, and prodded me to jump higher. No one before had ever examined my work so minutely, and I appreciate that tremendously. Erich Hobbing deserves my sincere appreciation, not only for his design and technology expertise but for indulging my obsessive-compulsive tendencies, permitting me to sit with him and suggest barely discernable adjustments in the art reproductions. John Fulbrook did a wonderful, tone-perfect cover, and I thank him for that. And my thanks to *New Yorker* cartoon editor Bob Mankoff for his encouragement and Ariel Bibby, Zach Kanin, and Patrick Seaton for their assistance in tracking and collecting the cartoons. I'm also grateful to Angela Gaudioso and the entire Creative Services Department at *The New Yorker* for their energetic support.

Of course, I send a huge, deafening round of applause to my fellow cartoonists, without whom this book simply would not have been possible. They are enormously talented, as you see, professionals who work at the highest level. I'm proud that they are my friends and grateful that they joined me in this project, particularly Frank Modell, from whom I'm still learning.

A special thought goes to my late brother-in-law, Howard, who blazed trails, down ski slopes and in so many other ways.

Last, but really first, I acknowledge my whole family and lifelong friends for their continuous support—particularly my sister, Judie, and cousin, Bert, who don't let me get away with anything. I especially thank my daughter, Lilia, who, in her commitment to save this planet, is a constant source of inspiration to me. And I thank my wife, Judith, who is always my best audience and cheerleader, but who went far above and beyond on this project, rereading everything countless times and sharing with me her sage intuitions, whether I wanted to hear them or not.

INDEX

George Booth, 5, 33, 88, 116, 125, 137–39

Roz Chast, 8, 35, 56, 77, 94, 126, 140–41
Frank Cotham, 17, 40, 74, 99, 131, 142–43
Leo Cullum, 4, 31, 58, 87, 108, 144–45

Matthew Diffee, 23, 47, 73, 109, 129, 146–47

Mort Gerberg, 20, 36, 52, 69, 84, 97, 111, 130, 135, 148–49
Sam Gross, 15, 39, 70, 93, 119, 150–51

J. B. Handelsman, 25, 45, 78, 96, 110, 152
Sidney Harris, 9, 29, 48, 67, 85, 103, 121, 153–54

Ed Koren, 18, 76, 105, 155–57

Glen Le Lievre, 27, 54, 133, 158–59
Arnie Levin, 10, 37, 59, 79, 101, 134, 160–61
Lee Lorenz, 6, 28, 43, 57, 71, 86, 100, 114, 128, 162–63

Marisa Acocella Marchetto, 26, 106, 164–65
Warren Miller, 12, 38, 60, 82, 104, 124, 166–67
Frank Modell, 3, 30, 41, 53, 68, 89, 107, 132, 168

Victoria Roberts, 11, 44, 81, 113, 169–70

David Sipress, 13, 46, 80, 118, 171–72
Barbara Smaller, 21, 49, 65, 98, 173–74
Mick Stevens, 19, 51, 92, 120, 175–76

Mike Twohy, 22, 55, 75, 117, 177–78

P. C. Vey, 7, 34, 64, 90, 115, 179–80

Kim Warp, 16, 42, 72, 95, 122, 181–82
Robert Weber, 14, 32, 50, 66, 83, 102, 123, 183–84
Gahan Wilson, 62–63, 185

Jack Ziegler, 24, 61, 91, 112, 127, 186–87

193